Portraits of
HINDUTVA

Rajesh Singh is a freelance analyst of politics and public affairs. He is a regular contributor to media platforms such as Wion News, Indus Scrolls and PGurus. He also writes for the leading think-tank, Vivekananda International Foundation, where he was a Visiting Fellow for a brief while. He had a nine-year stint with Delhi-based *The Pioneer* newspaper, where he served first as Deputy National Bureau Chief and later as Opinion Editor. He also served as Media Advisor to Goa Chief Minister Manohar Parrikar in 2002-03, during which period he was concurrently Director, Department of Information and Publicity, Government of Goa. He is now based in Delhi-NCR.

Portraits of
HINDUTVA

from Harappa to Ayodhya

RAJESH SINGH

RUPA

Published by
Rupa Publications India Pvt. Ltd 2018
7/16, Ansari Road, Daryaganj
New Delhi 110002

Sales Centres:
Allahabad Bengaluru Chennai
Hyderabad Jaipur Kathmandu
Kolkata Mumbai

ISBN: 978-93-5333-291-4

First impression 2018

10 9 8 7 6 5 4 3 2 1

Printed and bound by Parksons Graphics Pvt. Ltd., Mumbai

In memory of my parents

Hemlata Singh
and
Virendra Singh

Contents

Introduction

In writing this story of the evolution of Hindu identity from passive to active to assertive to aggressive, the first challenge was: Where does one begin? Initially, I toyed with the idea of beginning with the Bhakti period, because it was then that the Hindu faith was first demystified by common devotees who brought Bhakti into the personal space and popularized it among the masses with their innocent songs of surrender to god. These were common people, in the sense that they emerged from the ordinary class of society, and some were from the less-privileged and downtrodden sections. But these poet-devotees were extraordinary in their dedication to their personal gods—so much so that they themselves have gone down as saints. The Bhakti tradition also left, for Indian society, a rich legacy of folklore that continues to inspire people. It enriched literature too—Hindi, Marathi, Gujarati, Bengali, etc.

However, the ground for the Bhakti movement had been laid by the great saint-philosopher Ramanuja some two centuries earlier. It was Ramanuja who popularized the Vaishnavite movement, which later poets such as Surdas, Mirabai and Tulsidas participated in. So, it made sense to start with this Vaishnavite Dualist, or qualified Monist.

But then, Ramanuja could neither be studied nor understood without taking into account the philosophy he sought to reconstruct, if not reject altogether—that of Adi Shankaracharya. Indeed, if there is anything resembling an institution of Hindu faith and philosophical studies, it was set up by Adi

Shankaracharya in the form of four primary 'mutts' which exist in the country, each of which is headed by a Shankaracharya drawing spiritual lineage from the Adi Shankara. Besides, the first Shankaracharya had propagated the Hindu spirit like none before, through his nationwide tours and brilliant interpretations of the Vedas and the post-Vedic thoughts. He set the stage for Vedantic philosophy. Thus, no overview of a Hindu narrative could appear credible with an omission of the Adi's towering contribution. He also seemed to be the ideal starting point.

There was a problem, though, in settling on this solution. The country's foremost Hindu saint drew his inspiration from the Vedic age—and it was the Vedic era which set in place a plethora of rituals and beliefs, many of which are to this day defining characteristics of the Hindu faith. Additionally, given that the Rig Veda remains the most ancient and the most sacred of all Hindu literature, the span of time during which it was composed and promoted—which happens to be the Indus-Saraswati civilisation period—could not but be the mother of all beginnings.

Having thus tackled the question of beginning, the next challenge was to determine the close of the book. Of course, at one level there is no beginning or end to the Hindu story—Hinduism being Sanatana Dharma, eternal in its meaning and understanding. But the thread of Hindutva that runs through the narrative in the following chapters, at times identified by name, on occasions recognised in spirit, offered a solution. The demolition of the Babri Masjid in Ayodhya is seen by many as the high point of Hindutva—both in negative and positive terms, depending upon the individual's inclination. For both the pro- and anti-Babri camps, the monumental event which unfolded on 6 December 1992, had grown its roots many decades ago—even centuries ago. So, for want of a better alternative and driven by the compulsion to sustain focus on the book's recurring theme, the obliteration of the mosque has become the finale.

Three terms have been the subject of rousing debates and controversy: Hindu identity, Hindu nationalism, and Hindutva. The first and the third have existed since the Vedic period, though not by name to begin with. The contention that Hindutva is as old as the Vedic times is bound to be challenged by those who believe that Hindutva is a political term coined by hardline Hindu leaders, beginning with V.D. Savarkar. While it is true that Savarkar was arguably the first recorded person to have used 'Hindutva', it is also important to recollect that he considered Hindutva as the larger body, with Hinduism as one of the elements. In fact, he was dissatisfied with the term, 'Hinduism', on the ground that 'isms' do not help us accurately understand the Hindu faith, much less the concept of Hindutva. If his assertion is accepted, then Hindutva—in other words, 'elements' that make up the Hindu faith—certainly existed since the Vedic times. Political Hindutva, though, is of a more recent origin, with Bal Gangadhar Tilak using it with telling effect to counter the British rule, expose the political appeasement of the minority community, and challenge the aggressive conduct (as and when it occurred) of the Muslim population and its leaders in undivided India. Since then, political Hindutva has taken many shapes, at times in the hands of non-political organizations such as the RSS and the Vishwa Hindu Parishad, and often through the Bharatiya Jana Sangh and its successor, the Bharatiya Janata Party (BJP). In the process, Hindu nationalism and Hindutva have become intertwined to the extent that they are now indistinguishable from each other.

The mosque's demolition is seen by many of the protagonists as an assertion of both Hindutva and Hindu nationalism. The more moderate elements in that camp take gentle offence at the pejorative meaning that Hindu nationalism and Hindutva have acquired, arguing that being a Hindu and a nationalist is no crime; nor is it wrong to profess Hindutva leanings. After all, if it's fine to be Islamic in character, it is fine to believe in Hindutva as well. The argument is endearing in its simplicity but ground realities tell a different, often troubling, story on both sides. Ironically, the biggest damage to Hindutva/Hindu nationalism has come from some of its own over-zealous followers. That said, it is also mischievous of the opposing camp to demean anything Hindutva in nature. For instance, the word 'saffron' is pejoratively used by the anti-Hindutva lobby. Any talk of Hindu interests is instantly slammed as a 'majoritarian diktat', almost as if the Hindus have committed a crime by being in the majority. Opposition to Hindu nationalism/Hindutva ideology has led to the demonization of individuals like Savarkar and M.S. Golwalkar.

The conflict between pro- and anti-Hindutva groups acquired a new interpretation: It became a fight between secular and communal forces. It was a disingenuous attempt to, in one stroke, discredit the Hindu camp and brand it as communal. Those Hindu leaders who did not raise specific Hindu issues but spoke in circles were considered secular—by this definition, Tilak, Madan Mohan Malaviya, Rajendra Prasad, Vallabhbhai Patel and those of similar ideologies in the Congress became 'hardliners'; and Jawaharlal Nehru and his followers were not just 'moderates', but also 'secular'. If the communal tag was not bestowed on the former bunch, it was because those leaders were too big for even the formidable secular camp to take head-on.

The Nehru group found other ways—some indeed petty—to deal with them. But the secular camp went all out in its attacks on leaders of the RSS, the Hindu Mahasabha, and later the Jana Sangh and the BJP. The narrative received strength with the passage of time and the coming of the Nehruvian regime. Stung by the accusations of being communal and illiberal, the so-called pro-Hindu/anti-secular organizations finally questioned the concept of secularism itself—in the manner it has been understood and practised in India.

In an interview which has been reproduced in the book, *Hindu Nationalism: A Reader*, edited by Christophe Jaffrelot, L.K. Advani lashed out at critics and said: 'Even if Italy is called a Catholic state or Great Britain a Protestant one, they are still regarded as liberal. But if India is called a Hindu state, or a Hindu Rashtra, why does it become communal?' Referring to secularism in India, he said that the meaning of the term, as understood in the West, was separation of the powers of the State and the Church. In other words, it was a negation of theocracy, which had existed in the earlier centuries when the Papal authorities divided nations and regions between their trusted political rulers. Advani said India had never been a theocracy, and thus the Western model of secularism for this country did not quite fit the Indian cultural or political ethos. He floated the term, 'positive secularism', and elaborated that it meant the rejection of both minority appeasement and antipathy to anything Hindu.

The book also carries excerpts of a lecture Atal Bihari Vajpayee gave in 1992 on the subject. Interestingly, he delinked secularism from religion in the Indian context and said: 'Secularism means pertaining to the human existence in the present world, and it should be understood that it does not require any reference to religion. Secularism is different from religion, without religion or temporal.' During the course of his speech, Vajpayee said what is still often invoked by leaders of the BJP to explain secularism: 'I feel that had we translated the word "secular" as "sampradaya nirpeksha" or "panth nirpeksha", in the very beginning, many apprehensions would not have arisen. Whatever might have been the differences of opinion on the interpretation of the word "secular", all, however, agreed that the State should be non-communal.' These nuances have not found takers in the secular (or pseudo-secular) camps who maintain that semantics cannot wipe out the anti-minority taint from the face of the Right-wing organizations—and that, while one may identify secularism by any definition, such identification will not change the reality that the RSS and its affiliates are communal by nature.

While it continues to be fiercely debated among politicians whether the 'pseudo-seculars' or the 'communalists' have pursued a divisive agenda, the 'Hindu' issue did not even leave the judiciary untouched. A three-judge Bench of the Supreme Court, delivering its verdict, in December 1995, on a bunch of appeals which arose from decisions of the Bombay High Court, had set aside the High Court's order which had held certain politicians guilty under the Representation of the People Act, 1951, for invoking religion to attract votes. The apex court rubbished the claim that the invocation of Hindu or Hindutva by a candidate amounted to corrupt practice under the Act. It said: 'These Constitution Bench decisions, after detailed discussions, indicate that no precise meaning can be ascribed to the terms "Hindu", "Hindutva" and "Hinduism"; and no meaning in the abstract can confine it to the narrow limits of religion alone, excluding the content of Indian culture and heritage. It is difficult to appreciate how in the face of these decisions, the term "Hindutva" or "Hinduism" per se in the abstract, can be assumed to mean and be equated with narrow fundamentalist Hindu religious bigotry...' The Bench further observed that the use of those terms could well relate to a 'way of life' for Indians and to the 'Indian cultural ethos'. Towards the end of 2016, the Supreme Court refused to undo the 1995 verdict on a plea by social activist Teesta Setalvad, pointing out that the issue at hand was an examination of that which constituted corrupt electoral practices, and not a larger debate on Hindu or Hindutva. The 1996 verdict has been expectedly flayed by various activists—V.M. Tarkunde of People's Union of Civil Liberties (PUCL) called it a 'very severe blow to the principle of secular democracy'. Writing for the Left-oriented *Frontline* magazine, A.G. Noorani called the judgement 'flawed', and said one of the judges on the bench, Justice J.S. Verma, had jumped to an 'absurd conclusion' from an article by Maulana Wahiduddin Khan, that 'Hindutva' should be understood and used as 'synonym of "Indianisation"...'

The journey of Hindu identity and Hindutva had other important milestones, some of which are traced in this book. If Adi Shankaracharya provided the religious impetus and the Bhakti poets the devotional touch, those like Swami Vivekananda and Sri Aurobindo offered a spiritual-philosophical interpretation whose impact went beyond the shores of India. After Tilak, who was deeply influenced by these two gurus, the political use of Hinduism as a glue to bind people was carried forward by others, the most prominent among them being Golwalkar, Savarkar and Syama Prasad Mookerjee. Then came L.K. Advani and Bal Thackeray, almost rising at the same time on the Hindutva horizon. There was, however, another name that is less discussed in connection with the subject—Hanuman

Prasad Poddar. Most of us would ask, 'Poddar, who?' He was one of the founders of Gita Press, which is going as strong today as it had been nearly ninety years ago. Gita Press single-handedly crafted the Hindu consciousness of millions of Indians through the publication of the popular Hindu sacred books such as the Ramayana, the *Bhagavad Gita* and the Mahabharata, ensuring both quality and economy of pricing. Besides, Gita Press brought out the widely circulated *Kalyan* magazine that both reflected and shaped Hindu thoughts. Poddar played a major role not just in promoting Hinduism but also through his networking with several influential Hindu leaders cutting across political parties and non-political organizations, taking forward the Hindutva bandwagon.

The Hindutva project has, however, at best registered limited political gains for its protagonists. Barring rare occasions, such as at the height of the Ayodhya temple movement, the Hindus have not voted as a consolidated entity in favour of the BJP. Even in the 2014 Lok Sabha election and the 2017 Assembly election in Uttar Pradesh, the party's victories are attributed more to its positive message of change and development than to the Hindu identity factor. One main reason for the failure to convert Hindutva into electoral gains has been the caste divide within the community itself. By and large, the Scheduled Castes have been wary of being part of this grand grouping because of historical reasons. They have been victims of feudal caste politics for centuries and view the Hindutva movement as one driven by the privileged sections of the Hindu society, which had kept them at an arm's distance. Besides, they have had political options; in Uttar Pradesh, the Bahujan Samaj Party rose to heights on the foundation of Dalit support. Another division of Hindu votes happened when Prime Minister V.P.

Singh implemented the Mandal panel's report to provide reservation to Other Backward Classes within the community.

Hindutva leaders have been aware of this weak link in the chain and have been trying to address it. One reason why Tilak chose the Ganesh Chaturthi celebrations as a people's movement was because the festival saw the participation of all caste groups. The RSS has been working overtime to bridge the caste divide, realising that its dream of Hindu consolidation cannot be realised as long as such divisions remain. But it is finding difficulty in persuading the Dalit community to accept that it is not a brahminical organization. Hindu confluence in southern India has been even more of a challenge. Dravidian politics reigns in Tamil Nadu and it has kept Hindutva at bay. In Kerala, both the Congress party and the Left have readily aligned with pro-Muslim organizations to thwart the BJP's prospects, whereas in Andhra Pradesh and Telangana, local leaders and factors have provided no space for Hindutva to grow. In recent months, though, pro-Hindu outfits have begun to make their presence felt in Kerala.

No one book can do justice to the vast subject of Hinduism, Hindu identity, Hindu nationalism and Hindutva. There are far too many strands to count, let alone adequately grasp. And then there are varying and sharply conflicting opinions. This book is an attempt to offer an overview, nothing more and, hopefully, nothing less.

ONE

The Seed is Sown

Hear us, O Agni, in your common dwelling:
harness thy rapid car of Amrta.
Bring Heaven and Earth, the Deities's Parents, hither:
Stay with us here, nor from the Gods be distant.

R<small>IG</small> V<small>EDA</small>

In the beginning, there was no Hinduism or Hindutva. Or maybe there was; only that it was not known by any name. If Hinduism is a way of living, that way could not have developed suddenly with the arrival of the term; it must have been in a state of continuum, evolving as it journeyed. The Hindu faith was driven by Dharma, Karma and Samskara. But the origin of Hinduism, before even the Vedas were written and gods and goddesses existed and ruled our world, is considered by many to be in the realm of myth—and myth, as the venerable *Oxford English Dictionary* says in one of its definitions, is a 'widely held but false belief or idea'. This explanation is understandably repulsive to the Hindus. In any event, Hinduism is a definite reality and it must have an origin which is not a myth.

Scholars of Hinduism differ sharply on many aspects of the subject, but there is broad agreement on at least two points. The first is that the initial offshoots of what we today understand as the Hindu faith, sprung up during the Indus-Saraswati civilization. Author and academician Gavin Flood writes that the 'origins of Hinduism lie in two ancient cultural complexes, the Indus valley civilization which flourished from 2500 BCE to about 1500 BCE, though its roots are much earlier, and the Aryan culture which developed during the second millennium BCE.'[1] It is interesting that he keeps the issue of roots open-ended, because several academicians have strongly maintained that the civilization goes back many years further. Vedic scholar S. Kalyanaraman, who leaves little doubt in anybody's mind that he strongly believes in the direct linkage between the ancient civilization and the evolution of the Hindu faith as we know it today, even titled a series of scholarly papers on the subject which he edited, as the *Vedic River Saraswati and Hindu Civilization*.[2] Although less enthusiastic about a connect between the religious ideologies of the ancient period and Hinduism as we have come to understand it, anthropologist Rita P. Wright concedes, 'We have found that the association of gods and goddesses with natural phenomena and references to supernatural and animistic beings fall closely in line with Indus imagery and a deeply expressed impulse to break down and transform the natural world into a built world.'[3]

The second is that as terminologies, both Hinduism and Hindutva are modern-day constructs reflective of traditions and beliefs that millions of people in the Indian subcontinent shared since many centuries before the advent of Christ. First came the word Hindu, then Hinduism, and thereafter Hindutva in the popular narrative. Author and expert on Oriental studies,

[1] *An Introduction to Hinduism*; Gavin Flood; Cambridge University Press; Reprinted in 2014
[2] *Vedic River Saraswati and Hindu Civilization*; Edited by S. Kalyanaraman; Aryan Books International, 2008
[3] *The Ancient Indus: Urbanism, Economy, and Society*; Rita P. Wright; Cambridge University Press, 2010

Wendy Doniger, says a Hindu, for the Persians and the Arabs who lived in the fourth through eighth centuries BCE, was anyone who lived beyond the mighty Sindhu (or the Indus) river. It was an outsider's name for the people who inhabited the territory around the Indus River. 'The Persians called the region Hindustan.'[4] Academic Bansi Pandit writes that while the genesis of the term Hindu is 'somewhat controversial, the consensus among scholars is that as early as 500 BCE, the ancient Persians called the Indian people living on the banks of the river Indus (known as Sindhu in Sanskrit) as Sindhus. In the Persian language the word Sindhu became Hindu... The original name of the Hindu religion is Sanatana Dharma.'[5]

While the geographical interpretation of Hindu (and Hinduism as a consequence) has lost much of its relevance today, given that borders have changed dramatically since those ancient times and large tracts of 'Hindu land' have now metamorphosed into different nations where Hinduism does not hold pre-eminence, it remains a useful compass for us to bear in mind the historical perspective. Of late, it has become a handy tool for those who, with good intent or with an aim to irritate, take pains to remind the non-Hindus of India that they too are Hindus—in at least the geographical sense—and also culturally, since they share the ancestry of Indian Hindus. On a more ambitious scale, the concept of Hindu Rashtra (Hindu nation) is sought to be justified by the above arguments. For all these efforts, however, there are not too many takers even among the Hindu community, for this stretch of imagination. Yet, it cannot be denied that the Hindu cultural history is not

[4]*On Hinduism*; Wendy Doniger; Aleph Book Company, 2013
[5]*The Hindu Mind: Fundamentals of Hindu Religion and Philosophy for All Ages*; Bansi Pandit; New Age Books; Reprinted in 2014

merely a story of Hindus, but those of the other religious denominations as well, whether Indic or otherwise. Any attempt to disengage the non-Hindu narrative as being separate from the Hindu history is not just an exercise in futility but also an act of self-denial.

TRACING HINDUISM

Why is it so important that we trace Hinduism's beginning from the Indus-Saraswati civilization? This is because the civilization provides us with the most ancient evidentiary material that helps us deconstruct the Hindu journey. Scholars and academics, especially of the Left-Liberal kind, are scornful of anything they cannot see or feel. As an aside, even when they do see and feel, their interpretations are so divergent as to trigger conflicting opinions that leave us no closer to the truth. Nevertheless, such exercises are essential if only to keep the academic temperament alive and kicking. One instance of the obduracy in sections of the academia relates to what has been known the world over as the Indus Valley civilization for decades. Later-day experts have insisted on renaming it as the Indus-Saraswati civilization, much to the annoyance of the old guard dominated primarily by Leftist historians. Geological scientist K.S. Valdiya notes, 'More than 75 per cent of the 1,600 settlements of Harappan culture have been found in the valley of the Saraswati, such as at Banawali and Kalibangan in the Ghaggar valley and Ali Murad and Kot in the Hakra valley... The older Harappan sites are concentrated in the lower reaches of the Saraswati, while later Harappan settlements nestle in its upper reaches—in the Shivalik domain.'[6]

The resistance by a section of scholars to refer to the ancient

---

[6]*Vedic River Saraswati and Hindu Civilization*, Edited by S. Kalyanaraman, 2008

settlement as Indus-Saraswati civilization is motivated by certain factors. One, it would mean the acceptance of the existence of the river Saraswati. Two, it would lead to the acknowledgement of the fact that a real river has been mentioned in the Rig Veda, with a great amount of detail about its origin and flow. Three, it would blow away the theory these historians have held dear to their heart: That what is referred to as the Saraswati river is actually a river that flowed from Helmand in Afghanistan. And four, it would seriously jeopardise the long-held belief that dates the civilization and the Rig Veda to a period far recent than it actually may have been. The insistence on Indus-Saraswati civilization as against Indus Valley civilization is not a name-changing campaign guided by some misplaced sense of nationalism. That the Saraswati river existed; that it flowed into the northern and western plains; that a vast majority of findings of our ancient civilization has been along the banks of the river Saraswati; and that it dried out possibly due to tectonic shifts, are now generally accepted.

It is essential to come to terms with the reality of Saraswati, because this river is inextricably linked to the Hindu faith and to the journey of Hinduism from its civilizational roots. It cannot be forgotten that we know of the river Saraswati because of its mention—on more than one occasion, in glowing terms—in the Rig Veda, which is the most ancient sacred text of the Hindus. The troika of Hinduism-Rig Veda-Saraswati River can be neither ignored nor denied. Rig Vedic references indicate that Saraswati was a mighty river which sustained the ancient civilization across large parts of the land—and nurtured the concept of what came to be modern-day Hinduism. Not just that, the first Veda called the river 'Devitame'—a deity. There are more than 70 hymns in praise of the river in the Rig Veda. The 'Nadistuti Sukta' (hymn in praise of rivers) not just lavishes compliments on Saraswati for her prowess, but also locates her flow among the ten important rivers of the time.

'O Ganga, Yamuna, Saraswati, Shutudri (Sutlej), Parushini (Iravati, Ravi), follow my praise! O Asikni (Chenab) Marudvridha, Vitasta (Jhelum), with the Arjikiya (Haro) and Sushoma (Sohan), listen!'[7]

The river's mightiness is reflected in the following hymn:

'Sing a lofty song, for she is mightiest, most divine of streams
So, may Saraswati auspicious send good luck; she, rich in spoil, is never niggardly in thought
May we enjoy Sarasvan's (Saraswati's consort) breast, all beautiful, that swells with streams
May we gain food and progeny.'[8]

Now, it is possible for sceptics to dismiss rhetorical compliments and maintain that the composer of the lines had been imagining things or overreacting to some minor river which may not have been Saraswati at all. Indeed, this is exactly what certain historians have suggested. The identification of the Vedic river with the present-day Ghaggar-Hakra river was proposed by a bunch of scholars in the 19th and early 20th centuries, including Friedrich Max Muller and C.F. Oldham. More recent studies have confirmed those findings. However, Left-leaning historians have rejected the findings. One of them, Romila Thapar, termed the identification as 'controversial' and instead suggested that the river in question could have been a reference to a river of Helmand in Afghanistan.[9]

---

[7]*The Hymns of the Rigveda*; Ralph T.H. Griffith; Motilal Banarsidass Publishers, Reprinted in 2004
[8]ibid, Hymn XCVI
[9]*Early India: From the Origins to AD 1300*; Romila Thapar; University of California Press, 2002

But then, additionally, a great deal of scientific study has been done to understand the presence of river Saraswati and how it dried up. In Haryana especially, this campaign has been on for several years. Various scientific methods involving the use of multi-date and multi-resolution satellite imagery, GIS techniques, remote sensing means and ground data collection including soil studies, have managed to identify and study paleo as well as current channels of water that could have once been part of the now invisible river. Three experts, A.K. Gupta, B.K. Bhadra and J.R. Sharma had presented a detailed paper on the subject at a conference on the Vedic river in New Delhi in 2008, which made out a strong case for the existence of the so-called mythological river.[10] Various writers including Michel Danino have made compelling arguments in favour of the Saraswati River.[11]

The deep interlink between the Rig Veda and the river is one of sacredness for the Hindu, but the issue has also been a bone of contention between competing historians. Most Western academics—historians, Sanskritists et al—and the Left-Liberal grouping maintain that the Rig Veda was composed around 1500 BCE and that the Saraswati River (presuming its existence) had dried up by 1700 BCE. If the river had ceased to be nothing more than a weak stream by the time the Rig Veda came into being, how is it that the scripture refers to the Saraswati as the river of all rivers and demonstrates awe at its gushing power and its munificence? The composers had not exaggerated the flow of the Ganga or the Yamuna, so why would they seek out just the Saraswati for special treatment?

[10]*Vedic River Saraswati and Hindu Civilization*, Edited by S. Kalyanaraman, 2008
[11]*The Lost River: On the Trail of the Saraswati*; Michel Danino; Penguin Books India, 2010

The only sensible explanation would be that the Rig Veda was composed when the river was in full flow—and that would be well before 1700 BCE and during the height of river Saraswati's glory. The theory that the river was actually one that flowed from Afghanistan also does not reconcile with the following hymn in the Rig Veda: '*Ekachetat Saraswati nadinam suchir yati girbhya a samudram*'—meaning, that the river came down from the mountains and emptied itself in an ocean. While there are mountains in Afghanistan, where is the ocean there?

Besides, there is another problem with accepting that the Saraswati River was a figment of fertile imagination. How do we explain the genealogy of the Saraswat Brahmins? They are a sub-group of Brahmins, and while they can be found across the country, their concentration is mainly in the western and southern states of Maharashtra, Karnataka and Goa. The Saraswat Brahmins trace their ancestry to those who lived and worked in settlements on the banks of the river Saraswati, spreading knowledge and wisdom. As the Saraswati River began drying up and people started to leave the settlements, this community too followed suit. Initially, for reasons of contiguity, they moved to safer places in north India. Kalhana's 12th century classic, *Rajatarangini*, mentions the Saraswat Brahmins as one of the five Gauda Brahmins residing to the north of the Vindhya Range. Thereafter, this sub-group of Brahmins moved on to the west. A number of scholarly works on the subject have suggested that such a genealogy is indeed true.[12]

If the Saraswati River was one of the chief focus areas of the Rig Veda, then the Veda itself was the principal milestone of the ancient civilization. It is for this reason that the Indus-Saraswati

---

[12]'The Origin and Spread of Gauda Saraswats', S.V. Kamat, 1992; 'History of the Dakshinatya Saraswats', V.V. Kudva, 1972

civilization is also referred to as the Vedic period. Incidentally, it is the *Rig Veda*—along with many findings in excavations— that makes the civilizational era the most definitive starting point in deciphering the beginnings of Hinduism. 'The Veda as revelation is of vital importance in understanding Hinduism...'[13] In fact, it is critical to defining a Hindu. 'Sometimes, the Hindus defined themselves not by geography but by texts: We are the people whose canon is the Veda; or, we are the people who revere the Brahmins, the custodians of the Vedas.'[14] Of course, Hinduism being what it is, not every Hindu swears by the Rig Veda. Flood notes that 'its acceptance is not universal among Hindus and there are forms of Hinduism which have rejected the Veda and its legitimizing authority in the sanctioning of a hierarchical social order', adding also, by way of the scripture's importance nonetheless, that 'all Hindu traditions make some reference to the Veda, whether in acceptance or rejection...'[15]

Doniger finds means in addition to the Vedas to identify the Hindu entity, aware perhaps that the Veda is both a binding as well as a departing force within the Hindu community. She says, 'In general, though, Hindus have defined themselves not by beliefs, or even by geography, but by practices. The Hinduism of the Vedas was pluralistic. It advocated the worship (often through animal sacrifice) of a pantheon of many gods, most of whom by around 200 CE had been assimilated to Shiva, Vishnu in his many incarnations (including both Krishna and Rama) or the goddess in many forms...'[16]

---

[13]*An Introduction to Hinduism*, Gavin Flood, 2004
[14]*On Hinduism*, Wendy Doniger, 2013
[15]*An Introduction to Hinduism*, Gavin Flood, 2004
[16]*On Hinduism*, Wendy Doniger, 2013

DEFINING A HINDU

The fact is that it has been easier to find the roots of Hinduism, and its beginning, even in tentative ways, with the Indus-Saraswati civilizational period, than it has been to define a Hindu. Is a Hindu, one who holds the Vedic scriptures as sacred, to be followed both in letter and spirit? One who defies tenets of the Vedas, and yet retains faith in the pantheon of Hindu deities? One who affirms trust in the post-Vedic thoughts—the Vedantic philosophy? One who believes in form and qualities of deities (sagun) or in the formless (nirgun)? From Adi Shankara to Swami Vivekananda to Sri Aurobindo, saints and scholars alike have tried to unravel this mystery, but each has come up with different, if not always contradictory, versions. Equally important is the issue of practicality—can the teachings of our ancient texts be implemented in this new time and age? Swami Vivekananda put it succinctly at a speech he delivered in London in 1896: 'Theory is very good, indeed. But how are we to carry it into practice? If it be absolutely impracticable, no theory is of any value whatever, except as intellectual gymnastics. The Vedanta, therefore, as a religion, must be intensely practical. We must be able to carry it out in every part of our lives. And not only this, the fictional differentiation between religion and the life of the world must vanish, for the Vedanta teaches oneness—one life throughout.'[17]

Sri Aurobindo was equally pragmatic when he dismissed the heated campaigns to either promote or denigrate Hinduism through hollow methods. He said, 'There are many defenders and discoverers of truth now active among us. They are all busy defending, modifying, attacking, sapping or bolstering current

---

[17]*Reflections*; Swami Vivekananda; Om Books International, 2018

Hinduism. I am not eager to disparage but neither do I feel satisfied with any of them... There are the orthodox who are busy recovering and applying old texts or any interpretations, new or old, of these texts, which will support the existing order—and ignoring all that go against it. Their learning is praiseworthy and useful... but they do not seem to me to go to the heart of the matter. There are the heterodoxies who are busy giving new interpretations to old texts and institutions in order to get rid of all such features as the modern world finds it hard to assimilate... It is bringing to light or to a half light many luminous realities and possibilities... Still they do not seem to me to have the right grasp and discernment.'[18]

The heart of the matter in the observations of both these titans of Hindu religion and philosophy—and we shall return to them and others of their ilk later in the book—is that Hinduism cannot be and never has been straitjacketed. And this is what is to be seen and appreciated throughout the journey of the Hindu faith, beginning from the Indus-Saraswati civilization era. In later centuries, much after the Vedic period, Hinduism would pass through several challenges, from within and outside. But it remained resilient, bending once in a while for tactical reasons but rebounding too, and never breaking. It survived vicious onslaughts, often with rectitude and at times with controlled aggression, but maintained its primacy in the Indian region as the dominant religion. In the Vedic days, though, there were few such challenges and more of opportunities to give shape to what came to be known as Hinduism. Most of the modern-day practices of prayers and other rituals, of understanding the moral right and wrong, of determining ethical governance, and most

---

[18]*Essays Divine and Human: Writings from Manuscripts 1910-1950*; Sri Aurobindo; www.aurobindo.ru

importantly, of grasping a sense of pluralism, are attributable to that period. So, can we say with authority that the religious ideologies in the Indus-Saraswati period have a connection with the Hinduism of today?

THE LINK TO THE INDUS-SARASWATI CIVILIZATION

There are certain features which lead us in that direction. We have already seen the mention of various rivers in the Rig Veda (written during that era) which are considered sacred by Hindus today. There are the invocations to various deities— Indra, Agni, Surya, etc.—in the Veda that are now the staple diet of Hindu worshippers. The term 'Yug', which forms the time-basis of the majority faith in modern times, was used then as well. Excavations of the ancient civilizational site have produced various terracotta images which lend support to the argument that many practices and beliefs of inhabitants during the Vedic Indus-Saraswati period were similar to what we have today among the Hindu community. Structures have been unearthed that appear similar to sacred bathing places or temples which Hindus in later centuries constructed. The proposition is simple: If we insist that there is no specific linkage of modern-day Hindus with the traditions and beliefs of the Indus-Saraswati times, then we might as well conclude that our ancient civilization is dead and done with. That, happily, is not the case, even if a few of the connecting points may not withstand stringent academic scrutiny.

One of the chief proponents of such continuity has been B.B. Lal, who served as director-general of the Archaeological Survey of India and is regarded as an important voice on the subject. He insisted that there has been no break with our ancient cultural past.[19] In his inaugural address at an international conference on the Vedic River Saraswati and Hindu Civilization, Lal presented a number of instances drawn from findings of the excavations in the Indus-Saraswati belt, to illustrate his contention about continuity. A few of the more forceful ones from his address, 'The Saraswati: The Mother of Indian Civilization', are as follows:[20]

1. A terracotta figurine from Nausharo (part of the Harappan site), datable to 2800 BCE-2600 BCE, sports a red vermillion (sindoor) in the parting of her dark black hair. To this date, sindoor is applied by married Hindu women—though not all do so; some have the Mangalsutra.

2. The famous bronze figure of a dancing girl found at a mature Harappan period site in Mohenjo-Daro, wore spiralled bangles on the upper left arm. Women in Rajasthan and Haryana are seen even today to don similar bangles. Also at Mohenjo-Daro was found the figure of a woman wearing a gold cone, called 'chauk'— of the type that women in the above two states sport to this day.

3. A terracotta linga-cum-yoni figure excavated in Kalibangan, which dates to the Mature Harappan period. It has been identified with Shiva in the form of Pashupati, and points to the antiquity of the Shaivism order.

Then there are terracotta figurines in various yogic postures or asanas, again in the Mature Harappan period.

---

[19]*The Saraswati Flows On: The Continuity of Indian Culture*; B.B. Lal; Aryan Books International; 2002
[20]*Vedic River Saraswati and Hindu Civilization*, Edited by S Kalyanaraman, 2008

But there are experts who refuse to endorse the whole-hearted enthusiasm of the likes of B.B. Lal, although they are willing to admit to tentative linkages between the Vedic period beliefs and those of today. Anthropologist-academic Rita P. Wright is one such authority. In her book,[21] she says that although one has to rely 'on the architectural features and material culture believed to be devoted to religious practices, for example ritual objects, and imagery in which gods, goddesses, and mythological beings are depicted', these interpretations need a 'bridging framework to take us with greater confidence from the material world into the world of Indus ideological approach, in which better-known historical imagery and texts from present-day South Asian religions are applied to ancient remains from the Indus.' This involves the identification of ceremonial places and the study of terracotta figurines and masks, seals and tablets of the Indus-Saraswati period, as well as cross-cultural comparisons.

She also takes into account Sir Mortimer Wheeler's[22] conclusion that the 'Harappan mentality' anticipated the later religions—of which Hinduism was to be the prime. Pursuant to her studies, Wright believes that the 'lack of contextual evidence to confirm the use of specific buildings as temples or shrines leaves identification of religious structures in doubt.'[23] She then goes on to state that most of the materials discussed, especially the terracotta figurines (on which B.B. Lal has placed such confidence), were more likely objects 'owned and deployed by individuals'[24] and therefore less reflective of a socio-religious

---

[21] *The Ancient Indus: Urbanism, Economy, and Society*, Rita P Wright, 2010
[22] Sir Mortimer Wheeler was a 20th century British archaeologist who had intimately studied the ancient Indian civilization.
[23] *The Ancient Indus: Urbanism, Economy, and Society*, Rita P Wright, 2010
[24] ibid

order. But she does not shut out on the possibility of a certain amount of continuity. 'We have found that the association of gods and goddesses with natural phenomena and references to supernatural and animistic beings fall closely in line with Indus imagery and a deeply expressed impulse to break down and transform the natural world into a built world.'[25]

Regardless of the scholarly interpretations, the coincidences are too many to be brushed aside as accidental. The seeds of what we know as Hinduism were planted in the Indus-Saraswati period, nurtured by the waters of the Saraswati and nourished by the knowledge of the Rig Veda. It would be nearly 2,000 years later when Hinduism would proceed to the next level with the arrival of Adi Shankara. The seed would by then have sprouted into a sapling, waiting to break out from inhibitions and wanting to touch a greater number of lives. Meanwhile, in the intervening period that marked the demise of the ancient civilization and the first Shankara's arrival, the Rig Veda continued to be the guiding light in the formation of a loose religious structure.

[25]ibid

TWO

Creating a New Mould

Like the appearance of silver in the mother of pearls,
the world seems real until the Self,
the underlying reality, is realised.

ADI SHANKARACHARYA

The onward march of Hinduism would have certainly slackened, if not altogether halted, but for Adi Shankaracharya's timely intervention in the eighth century CE. This period was very unlike the centuries of Vedic India; challenges were emanating from new religions and from within the religious fold itself. Adi Shankaracharya lived for a mere 32 years, but in that short span of time, he elevated Hinduism to new heights and created a paradigm that would effectively serve to propagate and consolidate the Hindu faith in centuries to come. By any reckoning, he was the first Hindu reformer, besides being the first Shankaracharya. Shankara was a child prodigy and there are many stories revolving around him— naturally, they cannot be substantiated. But what he achieved certainly justifies the hyperbole associated with him. As we seek to understand his life, his contributions and his philosophy, we must not lose focus on his most enduring achievement: Constructing a new and robust Hindu narrative which not only exceeded the Vedic limits in interpretation but also sought to connect the common man with faith like never before. In that sense, Adi Shankaracharya was a revolutionary and a leader of a mass movement, a role which he excelled in through his extensive travels across the country. The Vedanta philosophy as we know it today is his gift to the Hindu community.

His revolution came not through the barrel of a gun or the tip of a sword, unlike in the happenings in Europe during roughly the same period. Charlemagne, or Charles the Great, was on a rampage, uniting much of central and eastern Europe as part of a Christendom bloc. He was later canonized by the Pope for his efforts. He led incursions in Muslim Spain and also converted the Saxons on the threat of death. The Massacre of Verden remains a telling, though a shameful reminder, in the history of forceful initiation of people into the Christian order and the decimation of the reluctant. More than 4,500 Saxons lost their lives in the process in Verden, which is now part of Germany. A thousand years later, sympathetic scholars tried to exonerate Charlemagne of the crime by churning out distorted literature. Later, he became a hero for Nazi Germany and its leader, Adolf Hitler. Pater Europae (The Father of Europe), as he came to be called for uniting much of the continent, ruled for 13 years with an iron fist. By contrast, Adi Shankaracharya didn't have a kingdom, but he reigned over the hearts of millions and brought lasting changes without recourse to force. He reshaped Vedic beliefs without denouncing them. The Vedantic stream of thought he initiated did not seek to break from the past; he only insisted that the post-Vedic period had to be fashioned in keeping with the times. Thus, his Vedanta was not a rejection of the Veda—it was a new opportunity to recalibrate the Vedic spirit. It was a path that would be tread in later centuries by leading Hindu saint-philosophers such as Swami Vivekananda and Sri Aurobindo and philosopher-teacher S. Radhakrishnan.

Virtually no branch of Hindu faith remained untouched by his influence.

There is no precise information on his date or place of birth, though it is generally accepted vide available material that he 'was born in the eighth century CE in the Malabar region of what is now Kerala.'[1] A popular story in circulation is that Shiva came to Shankara's parents in their dreams and asked whether they would want a son with a long but ordinary life, or one with a short but virtue-filled life. The parents were no doubt confounded by the choice, but eventually chose the latter. The son born was promptly named Shankara, after Shiva. Having reconciled to their child's short life-span in this world, they were overjoyed that Shiva had kept his other promise: Bestowing the child with virtuous, almost superhuman qualities. Shankara had mastered the four Vedas by the age of eight and was firmly placed to begin a journey which no ordinary eight-year-old could hope to undertake even if the desire had been there. But when the child announced his decision to take sanyaas, his by now widowed mother was heart-broken. She had been ecstatic at having a virtuous boy, but she was not willing to lose him to a different, spiritual world. She could not comprehend the cause; after all, Shankara was just a child and nothing tragic had happened to have triggered in him the desire for renunciation. But, he had his way finally. The incident that had a profound influence on him and shaped his rebellious outlook towards ritualism came sometime later when he returned home on hearing of his mother's demise. The Brahmins there refused to let him perform the final rites on the ground that a sanyaasi who had renounced his family could not do so. Shankara was born to a Brahmin family himself.

---

[1]*Incarnations: India in 50 Lives*; Sunil Khilnani; Penguin Allen Lane, 2016

There is another story surrounding his decision to take sanyaas. As a child, he had once accompanied his mother for a bath in the village river. Just as he took a plunge in the water, he cried out to his mother that a crocodile had caught hold of his legs and was dragging him down. He cried out, 'O dear mother! A crocodile is dragging me down. I am lost. Let me die peacefully as a sanyaasin. Give me your permission now.'[2] The distraught mother relented, and the crocodile let him go. Shankara's quest for a greater meaning in life began hereafter. He set out in search of a guru and found one in Swami Govindapada Acharya at an ashram in Badrinath. Swami Govinda taught him the philosophy of Advaita, which he himself had learnt from his guru Gaudapada Acharya.[3] These teachings were to change the complexion of the Hindu faith in the coming months, once Adi Shankaracharya embarked on his nationwide spiritual wandering and produced one remarkable interpretation and intellectual discourse after another on the sacred texts.

ADI SHANKARA ARRIVES

Those were the days of spiritual giants who professed their own philosophies and clashed often with rivals in the field, seeking to outdo them through debates and discussions. It was generally the case that the loser would not just accept defeat, but also convert to the rival's school of thought. Shankara had to overcome this challenge before he could be taken seriously by the elite class of spiritualists, let alone be accepted by the general public. The story that follows is especially relevant because it came to demonstrate the effectiveness of Shankara's

---

[2]www.hindupedia.com
[3]ibid

persuasive powers, fortified by his deep understanding of the scriptures, which was to later mesmerize millions of people. He was considered a greenhorn and his youthful appearance did not help matters. His clash with the venerable Mandana Mishra is the stuff that legends are made of, and it turned the young Shankara, almost overnight, into a respected and known figure in the hallowed world straddled by spiritual and religious leaders. While searching for his opponent in a town in what is now Madhya Pradesh, he came across the man's big house, 'where parrots could be heard chanting Vedic mantras'.[4] He barged into the house uninvited and, after exchanging insults with the great owner of the house by way of introduction, settled down for a debate. The question as to who would arbiter the result was quickly resolved; Mandana Mishra's wife, herself a scholar of some repute, would do the needful. She placed a garland of fresh flowers around the neck of each of the two contestants and declared that the garland which faded first would indicate the loser. This was a clever means she employed to remain neutral, considering that she had a vested interest.

But why had Adi Shankaracharya chosen the powerful Mandana Mishra? The sub-plot is as follows: The Purvamimamsa school, which vehemently promoted strict adherence to rituals as laid down by the sacred texts, was one of the most respected at that time. It had a huge following, no doubt helped by the fact that few people would dare to openly take on the powerful religious-spiritual leaders of this established institution. 'Shankara realised that unless he was able to win over the powerful rival, his goal of spiritually re-unifying India would remain difficult to fulfil.'[5] He decided to confront the

---

[4]*Incarnations: India in 50 Lives*, Sunil Khilnani, 2016
[5]www.speakingtree.in

foremost leader of this sect, Kumarilla Bhatta of Prayag, in what is now Allahabad. But when he arrived at Bhatta's house, the sect's leader was in the process of self-immolation as repentance for the sin he had committed of pretending to be a Buddhist and learning Buddhism's methods to eventually counter them. Shankara tried in vain to stop the act, but before dying Bhatta told the young ascetic about his disciple Mandana Mishra and suggested that he should meet him, since Mishra was indeed the most renowned proponent of the Purvamimamsa faith.[6]

Returning to the contest, the battle of wits went back and forth between Mandana Mishra and Shankara for 18 days. Finally, the flowers in the garland around Mishra wilted and he conceded defeat. But his shrewd wife was not done yet. She presented a fresh challenge to the victor, asking him to debate her on the art of love and see if he could prevail. She claimed that a husband can be considered defeated only if the wife too faces defeat. She reminded Shankara that the sacred texts held that the wife formed one-half of the husband's being. This was hitting below the belt, because Shankara, while an expert on the sacred texts and capable of revolutionary interpretations, had no understanding of the subject he was being called upon to deliberate. Not to be outdone, he sought time, which was granted. He then used his supreme yogic powers and 'entered the body of a king, proved to be a quick student at gathering the necessary knowledge, and returned to claim victory.'[7] Needless to add, both Mandana Mishra and his wife became the Shankara's disciples from thereon. He was to gather many more students and converts to the Vedantic thought process along the way.

[6]ibid
[7]*Incarnations: India in 50 Lives*, Sunil Khilnani, 2016

Scintillating as they may have been, Adi Shankaracharya's miracles—when the crocodile released him on hearing he would renounce the material world, or in the contest with Mandana Mishra's wife in preparation for which he entered a dying king's body—are just footnotes when compared to his titanic achievement in reconstructing the faith of the majority, and showing them a new and even more inclusive method to gain spiritually. The Advaita Vedanta, which binds Hindus together and which helped withstand many assaults on their religion over the past centuries, is Adi Shankaracharya's enduring contribution to the faith. It is both easy and difficult to understand Adi Shankaracharya. Easy because he was clear-headed about his mission: Unite the nation spiritually. And difficult, because he was, in the words of Jawaharlal Nehru, 'a curious mix of a philosopher and a scholar, an agnostic and a mystic, a poet and a saint, and in addition to all this, a practical reformer and an able organizer.'[8]

A popular theory patronized by a section of over-zealous enthusiasts is that Adi Shankara effectively arrested the growth of Buddhism in India. This is not borne out from historical evidence, for the reason that Buddhism's decline had preceded the Hindu saint-reformer's advent; most accounts say that the downward swing was most evident at least 100 years before Adi Shankaracharya came into the scene, and there are many reasons for that (which are outside the scope of this book). Suffice it to say that both internal and external factors contributed to the phenomenon that picked up steam between 400 BCE and 700 BCE.[9] Some experts have still insisted that one of the main

---

[8] *The Discovery of India*; Jawaharlal Nehru; Penguin Books India, Reprinted 2004
[9] *Merriam-Webster's Encyclopedia of World Religions*; Edited by Wendy Doniger; Merriam-Webster, 1999

causes had been the belligerent spread of Islam in later years. 'From 986 CE, the Muslim Turks started raiding northwest India from Afghanistan, plundering western India early in the eleventh century. Forced conversions to Islam were made, and Buddhist images smashed, due to the Islamic dislike of idolatry. Indeed in India, the Islamic term for an "idol" became budd.'[10] Nehru too pointed out that Buddhism 'had shrunk in India even before Shankara's time'.[11] And yet, it must be recognized that Buddhism was not finished in Adi Shankaracharya's era. It is possible that he had to face it as an opponent to the Hindu scriptures which he held dear. It can perhaps be said with some amount of caution that Adi Shankaracharya's brilliance and his deep connect with not just scholars but also the people at large, something which he achieved during his marathon voyage across the country, meeting people of all sects and beliefs, played a role in maintaining the dominance of Hinduism—which had been strongly hit in the immediate centuries following emperor Ashoka's reign—in the region.

The irony here is that Adi Shankaracharya has at times been called, half-jokingly and on occasions with derision, a closet Buddhist for his monastic ways and the establishment of monastic institutions—the four primary 'mutts'—in the country. 'Some of Shankara's Brahmin opponents called him a disguised Buddhist. It is true that Buddhism influenced him considerably.'[12] This is not the place to meander into the details of such 'accusations', but it is possible that, knowingly or unknowingly—the former perhaps, given that the Advaita philosopher was well-tuned to the spiritual happenings of

---

[10]*The Discovery of India*, Jawaharlal Nehru, 1946
[11]ibid
[12]ibid

his time—he had formulated the Monistic doctrine of maya corresponding to the Buddhist thoughts on the subject. But, on the other hand, Adi Shankara, keeping with the same Monistic belief, spoke of the Atman, which is far removed from Buddhist teachings. Indeed, most Buddhist traditions trash the premise of a permanent and unchanging Atman (Self, Soul), which is a pre-Buddhist concept popularized through the Upanishads. 'The Nikaya texts of Buddhism deny that there is anything called the Atman that is the substantial absolute or essence of a living being, an idea that distinguishes Buddhism from the Brahmanical (proto-Hindu) traditions.'[13] The biggest disclaimer of his Buddhist leanings becomes evident from a passage in one of the Shankara Vijayas, chronicles of the life and teachings of the first Shankaracharya, which informs that Shankara had continued his 'merciless refutation of all hostile creeds and philosophies—the teachings of the Tathagata (Buddha) became lifeless, the school of Kumarila became silent, the Naiyayika philosophy became weak and paralysed, and the Kapila's system also followed suit.'[14] Whatever the case may have been, to contextualize Adi Shankaracharya's teachings in a narrow Buddhist narrative is to potentially undermine his enormous contribution to the consolidation of the Hindu faith.

UNIFIER OF HINDU FAITH

Shankara's approach can best be grasped by understanding the backdrop in which it came. For centuries since the Vedic period, the Hindu faith as it evolved was heavily centred

---

[13]*The Selfless Mind: Personality, Consciousness and Nirvana in Early Buddhism*; Peter Harvey; Routledge, 2013
[14]*Incarnations: India in 50 Lives*, Sunil Khilnani, 2016

on the Vedas and the strict adherence to rituals these texts proposed. Besides, Vedic literature was not accessible to the masses, either because the common man did not possess the literary intellect to understand it, or because he was discouraged from pursuing the sacred texts, which were the exclusive preserve of the Brahmins. Popular forms of worship from the Vedic era onward had limited the quest for a greater spiritual understanding among the faithful. As the community grappled with these challenges, the rise of Buddhism, especially during emperor Ashoka's rule as part of the Maurya dynasty in the third century BCE, brought forth a new dimension—since it disputed many of the Vedic practices and attempted to create a more broad-based understanding of spirituality and the relatively easier participation of the ordinary individual in that effort. Although Buddhism's influence had significantly tapered off by the time Adi Shankaracharya came, many of its tenets had left a mark on the Hindu faithfuls. The task was, therefore, cut out for Adi Shankaracharya. He needed to revitalize and reform through an entirely new construct without fully dismissing the old. It was a tight-rope walk which only an intellectual giant of Shankara's proportions could manage.

At the core lay the onerous work of making common sense of the complex pantheon of scriptures. 'Shankara's ambition as a thinker was to provide a unified, coherent reading of the great plurality and diversity of the Hindu scriptures.'[15] But the great teacher-saint's idea of unity was even grander. He wanted to break the barriers of language too, across the country. He knew of the linguistic obstacles that he would have to deal with vis-à-vis the north and the south, and he wanted to break

---

[15]Jonardon Ganeri, Professor of Philosophy, Arts and Humanities, New York University.

them. 'It would seem that Shankara wanted to add to this sense of national unity and common consciousness.'[16] Adi Shankara proposed two theories: That the Soul and the Self were one and the same (Atman); and that all the apparent distinctions were illusory (Maya). And he went about explaining them with an intellectual sharpness that was his hallmark: 'I am neither earth nor water nor fire nor air nor sense organ nor the aggregate of all these... I am neither above nor below, neither inside nor outside, neither middle nor across...for I am indivisible, one by nature, all pervading like space.'[17] The one sacred text he decided to make the focus of his intellectual pursuit was the Upanishad series. Out of these efforts emerged the philosophy of Advaita Vedanta.

The Upanishads are said to have been composed from around 800 BCE to 400 BCE—some even before—but they had lived in the shadows of the Vedas for centuries. Their 'rediscovery' by Adi Shankaracharya instantly promoted the scriptures to centre-stage. They are a collection of writings gleaned from the oral transmission which comprised the four Vedas, and can thus be considered an extension of the original. And yet, there is something refreshingly different in them, enough to make the body of work the core of Indian philosophy. Perhaps Adi Shankaracharya was the first major Hindu guru to have appreciated the value of the Upanishads, but he was not to be the last. Swami Vivekananda, Sri Aurobindo and S. Radhakrishnan were hugely impressed and influenced by them. Sri Aurobindo held the Upanishads to be the 'supreme work of the Indian mind' and 'evidence of a unique mentality

---

[16]*The Discovery of India*, Jawaharlal Nehru, 1946
[17]*Incarnations: India in 50 Lives*, Sunil Khilnani, 2016

and unusual turn of spirit.'[18] For Swami Vivekananda, Vedanta and the Upanishads were inseparable to the extent that 'this Vedanta, the philosophy of the Upanishads, I would make bold to state, has been the first as well as the final thought on the spiritual plane that has ever been vouchsafed to man.'[19] Shankara's choice of using the Upanishads as the core of his philosophical outlook was interesting for two reasons. One, he signalled his intent to not make a complete break away from the Vedas—since the Upanishads contain ideas and expositions that formed the later part of the Vedic oral tradition. Two, even while doing so, he made it known that the Upanishads were an 'alternative', so to say, for those who had issues with the Vedas over their rigid teachings. The non-dualist or monist concept came from Adi Shankaracharya's study and creative interpretation of the Upanishads. His critics would snigger that Shankara favoured monism because he could not count beyond one.

The Vedantic school of thought which Adi Shankaracharya pioneered, and which continues to form the backbone of Hinduism to this day, was enlarged some 300 years later by theologian-philosopher Ramanuja. A Brahmin like Shankara, he was considered to be the closest to Adi Shankaracharya in intellect and spiritual understanding of the sacred texts. His contribution was two-fold. The first is that he challenged Shankara's monism concept and insisted on duality—or at best, qualified monism—'Vishishtadvaita'. The second is that he was an exponent of the Vaishnavism tradition, in contrast to Shankara's Shaivism. It is interesting that since the Vedic era,

[18]*The Foundations of Indian Culture*; Sri Aurobindo; Sri Aurobindo Ashram Publications Department, 1998
[19]*Reflections*, Swami Vivekananda, 2018

Shiva occupied a prime spot in Hindu religious matters, and it was Ramanuja who brought Vishnu in the reckoning. There is no doubt that Ramanuja helmed the dualist movement. 'You will be astonished if you compare Ramanuja and his work with the other dualist Vaishnava sects in India, to see how they resemble each other in organization, teaching, and method. There is the great south Indian priest Madhva Muni, and following him, our great Chaitanya of Bengal...'[20]

THE OTHER GREAT SAINT, RAMANUJA

Ramanuja was a staunch proponent of Bhakti, or devotion to a personal god—in his case, Vishnu. Ramanuja's initial learning was in the Advaita Vedantic tradition, with Yadava Prakasa as his teacher. But he disagreed strongly and frequently with the concept of monism and eventually teacher and pupil went their own separate ways.[21] He went on to write many important interpretational texts on the Brahma Sutras and the *Bhagavad Gita* as well. Unlike Shankara, he started off as an ordinary householder, even getting married. But spirituality drew him away from marital life and he became a monk. As with Shankara, there are miraculous stories involving Ramanuja. It is said that he once tried to meet a renowned Advaita scholar of the 11th century CE, but could not because the scholar died before the rendezvous. However, the corpse of the scholar, named Yamunacharya, rose from the dead to declare Ramanuja as the leader of the Vaishnava sect. Like all such narrations, this one too remains apocryphal. Even his marriage is in the grey area

---

[20]ibid
[21]'Ramanuja: Hindu Theologian and Philosopher', J.A.B. van Buitenen, *Encyclopaedia Brittanica*, 2008

of history. The problem of distinguishing truth from fiction becomes almost insurmountable in the case of legends because of the enormous amount of hagiographic accounts that have surfaced over the decades and centuries about these figures.

What is known is that Ramanuja became a priest at a temple in Kanchipuram (Tamil Nadu), where he taught that moksha, or liberation, cannot be achieved through devotion to the nirgun (formless) deity or through monism, but with the assistance of a personal god—and that god would be Vishnu—and through the concept of duality. He said, 'Dualism is the natural idea of the senses; as long as we are bound by the senses we are bound to see a god who is only personal, and nothing but personal, we are bound to see the world as it is.' For all his enormous contribution to the advancement of Hindu faith, Ramanuja is generally treated as secondary to Adi Shankaracharya. This perception has got nothing to do with the scale and depth of his work, which remains second to none. It is perhaps due to the historical fact that Shankara founded the Vedantic order and Ramanuja added variety to it through the introduction of Vaishnavism, that the former gets the pride of place. But, as pioneer to pioneer, Ramanuja was as much of it as Adi Shankaracharya. Together, though working in different centuries, they shaped Vedanta, so much so that Swami Vivekananda remarked that 'the people who call themselves Hindus had better be called Vedantists,' regardless of the dualist or monist leanings they may prefer.

Ramanuja's emphasis on Bhakti embellishes his reputation as a pioneer. His work can said to be a precursor to the Bhakti movement which seized the country between the 15th century CE and the 18th century CE. The Bhakti tradition followed along the lines of Ramanuja's belief that there needs to be a personal god to see humankind through, and that personal god has to have qualities and form. And so, a variety of personal gods ranging from Shiva to Vishnu to Krishna to Ram to the goddess Shakti, were to become the fulcrum of the Bhakti saints. It was an eclectic tradition in that the saint-devotees were drawn from all strata of life—from the marginalized to the royalty, and from the uneducated to the privileged class.

The Bhakti movement would be the next milestone in the advancement of the Hindu faith, a faith that gets up close and personal and is unencumbered by the dogmas of scriptures and their weighty interpretations. The time for intellectual gurus and dazzlers of spirituality to make way for the 'rest' was to come soon.

THREE

The Bards Make a Revolution

If you want the truth, I'll tell you the truth.
Listen to the secret sound,
the real sound,
which is inside you.

KABIR

The Bhakti movement did not start as an orchestrated campaign. Different poets began composing in different decades, at different locations, in different languages. Their poetries were differently framed, at times merely lyrical, at moments profoundly literary. They addressed different gods in different ways. The poets would at times break down in despair, and on occasions, their hopes in their god would soar so high that they would indulge in praiseful exaggeration. Often, in fits of anger and frustration, they would even castigate their deity for failing to rescue them in times of crisis. But there were commonalities too. The Bhakti poets sang—most of them at least. They wrote and sang in languages other than Sanskrit, which had until then been the dominant medium. They travelled extensively—most of them—and their words and expressions were down-to-earth and thus appealed to the lowest common denominator. For them, faith in their personal god was blind, unwavering and unquestioning; most did not engage in philosophical nuances. And so, they stood out from saint-philosophers of the past. Although they did not work in tandem, taken together their outpouring of trust gave a new direction to Hindu religion, bringing it to the doorsteps of the believer. Given the manner in which it connected people from all walks of life, it would not be out of place to term it a mass socio-religious movement of the kind Hinduism had not seen before.

However, there are postmodern scholars who hold that the phenomenon has been mis-contextualized as a social reform movement. They contend that the scriptures of the Bhakti tradition were still the old ones—the Vedas, Upanishads, and Puranas. They claim that all that the Bhakti poets did in their various ways was to decontextualize and reconstruct the old Vedic texts.[1] They believe there was nothing spectacularly new in the Bhakti tradition. 'But for all its sophistication, this "modernized" Bhakti was still unable to overcome the older tradition.'[2] Those such as Madeleine Biardeau and Jeanine Miller agree with this assertion and say that Bhakti was a continuation of, and the expression of, old ideas found in the Vedas and Upanishads.

But many others differ with this interpretation, saying that the Bhakti cult had challenged the hegemony of Sanskrit, rigidity in traditions and the need to adopt certain 'norms' in pursuing faith. One prominent Indian scholar maintained that the Bhakti movement was a sort of Kshatriya reform of a Brahmin religion.[3] This has been contested by recent researchers who state that it was neither a rebellion against the Brahminical order nor a rejection of Sanskrit.[4]

---

[1] *The Embodiment of Bhakti*; Karen Pechilis Prentiss; Oxford University Press, 2000
[2] Ranajit Guha, academician and leading author on subaltern studies.
[3] Ramakrishna Gopal Bhandarkar, historian and teacher, in whose memory the Pune-based Bhandarkar Oriental Research Institute is named.
[4] *The Language of the Gods in the World of Men*; Sheldon Pollock; University

Interestingly, some scholars who profess the theory that the Bhakti tradition was indeed a reformatory one, have sought to construct an analogy between it and the Protestant movement, which positioned itself squarely in contradiction to the Catholic faith. One of them was Monier Monier-Williams. But since he is best remembered for his book which predicted the demise of Hinduism as a consequence of Christianity's rise in India, his comparison must be taken with a pinch of salt.[5] He also dealt a self-blow to his credentials by admitting that 'Englishmen are too practical to study a language very philosophically.'[6] In any case, the Bhakti movement was triggered by situations that were Indian in nature, and similarities, if any, with the likes of the Protestant faith, should be considered merely incidental.

We need to understand here that the Bhakti poets were not rejecters of the Hindu faith, and it was, therefore, natural for them to generally not denounce the sacred scriptures. The fact that they found new ways to interpret the religion without disturbing the old order is the real accomplishment. In any case, the Hindu belief would have gone nowhere with an outright dismissal of the Vedic past or the various scriptures that have come to be associated with the faith. Considering that the Bhakti movement was an important landmark in the long and eventful journey of Hinduism, it would be more relevant to have a core understanding of the term 'Bhakti', and realize the causes of the tradition, its various strands, and its impact on the socio-religious aspects of Hindu belief. At one level, Bhakti was an expression of individualized internal feelings; at

---

of California Press, 2006

[5]*Hinduism*; Monier Monier-Williams; Pott, Young, & Co., 1878. Monier-Williams was a scholar of great repute.

[6]*Scholar Extraordinary: The Life of Professor the Rt. Hon. Friedrich Max Muller, P.C.*; Nirad C Chaudhuri; Chatto & Windus, 1974

another, it was a manifestation of a collective sigh for change. To this day, Bhakti songs spring up from public platforms, from temple premises, from films, and through folklore. Bhakti renderings have become an intrinsic and inseparable part of everyday life and traditions of the ordinary Hindu. In the true sense, the Bhakti movement has been the 'greatest religious revolution that India has ever seen, (and made religion) no longer a thing of knowledge but of emotion.'[7] Hazariprasad Dwivedi[8] had expressed a similar sentiment, but he was more specific in saying that it was even greater than the Buddhist movement—'*Baudh dharm ke andolan se bhi adhik vishal.*'[9]

BHAKTI AS SEEN BY ACADEMICS

There have been several English language Orientalists, both Indian and Western, who have done seminal work in helping us appreciate the Bhakti trend. However, they have often faced an insinuation that their interpretations have failed to grasp the unique Indianness that permeated the Bhakti movement, and also that quite a few of them infused extraneous factors to embellish their own ideological leanings. It is, therefore, necessary to look beyond the body of work in English—not so much to discredit the English language writers but to gain a more holistic understanding of a phenomenon that has left an indelible mark on not just the Hindu faith but on Indian

---

[7] *Encyclopedia of Religion and Ethics* (George Abraham Grierson); Edited by James Hastings; 1908-27
[8] Hazariprasad Dwivedi was a 20th century Hindi litterateur. He is known for his historical research on the Bhakti movement and its impact on society. His study of Bhakti poet Kabir is considered a masterpiece.
[9] *Hindi Sahitya: Udbhav aur Vikas*; Hazariprasad Dwivedi; Rajkamal Prakashan, Twenty-first Edition, 2017

literature itself. Indeed, even the English commentators have themselves fallen back often on vernacular writings. Dwivedi remains on top of that vernacular list, being quoted extensively. 'Owing to his vivid prose style, Dwivedi's influence was hardly confined to an academic context.'[10] His Hindi Sahitya ki Bhumika and Hindi Sahitya: Udbhav aur Vikas are standards texts of academic reference. The other writer who is rated just a notch below Dwivedi is Acharya Ramchandra Shukla,[11] who conducted a deep study of the Bhakti trends ranging from nirgun to sagun to Sufi, and the Vaishnavite tradition of poetry. It can be said without fear of exaggeration that no serious understanding of the Bhakti movement is possible without invoking the works of both Dwivedi and Shukla.

Returning to the theme of Indianness mentioned earlier, English translations of Sanskrit-origin words, especially relating to religion and spirituality, at times tend to go off-track or end up as misinterpretations or result in part-understanding. The failure has not only cast doubts on literary efforts but also promoted a narrative of what it should be seen as, as opposed to what it really is. True, such obfuscation is sometimes deliberate, driven by the author's personal slant, but often it is to do with a genuine shortcoming. The translation of 'Bhakti' too has the potential to lead the attempter into a frustratingly unclear world of semantics. 'The word "Bhakti" is notoriously hard to translate. The Sanskrit "Bhakti" is an action noun derived from the verbal root "bhaj"— meaning, broadly to "share, to possess", and occupies a semantic field that embraces the notions of belonging, being loyal, even

---

[10]*A Storm of Songs: India and the Idea of the Bhakti Movement*; John Stratton Hawley; Harvard University Press, 2017

[11]Acharya Ramchandra Shukla, credited with having written the first chronological history of Hindi literature. His books on the Bhakti poets Surdas, Kabir and Tulsidas are considered must-reads.

liking. References to Bhakti by the grammarian Panini reveal this range of meanings in the fourth century BCE, but suggests that even then the word's most important usage was in the domain of religion.'[12] The concept of 'sharing' as a definition of Bhakti too has been much discussed, with 20th century Indologist J.A.B. van Buitenen pointing out that it evolved into 'declaring for, choosing for'. So, did the word Bhagvan come from Bhakti, or was it the other way around? In any case, it is clear that Bhakti means devotion for all practical purposes, and that the devotion is directed at a personal god. Swami Vivekananda had done a much-quoted English translation of the *Narada Bhakti Sutra*, wherein Bhakti was referred to as 'intense love for god', and the Bhakti saint, 'giving up all refuge, takes refuge in god'. The Sutras also stated (in his translation) that Bhakti is 'greater than Karma, greater than gyan or Raj Yoga even.'

Before we go any further, it must be kept in mind that while Ramanuja had laid the (theological/populist) ground for the Bhakti movement, the link between the Vaishnava guru and the Bhakti era was Ramanand, a fourteenth-century saint and devotional philosopher. Inspired by Ramanuja, he counted among his disciples leading Bhakti poets such as Kabir and Ravidas.[13] It has so turned out that the disciples have become more known than the teacher! His thoughts are said to have influenced the establishment of Sikhism, and they find reference in the holy Sikh scripture the Adi Granth.[14] Hazariprasad Dwivedi mentions him as among the two scholars (the other being Mahaprabhu Vallabhacharya) who were the most

---

[12]*A Storm of Songs*, John Stratton Hawley, 2015
[13]*Who Invented Hinduism?: Essays on Religion in History*; David N. Lorenzen; Yoda Press, 2006
[14]*The Hagiographies of Anantadas: The Bhakti Poets of North India*; Winand Callewaert; Curzon, 2000

responsible for re-energizing the flow of the Bhakti stream in north India.[15] Ramanand was a rare mix of nirgun and sagun—he was a Ram Bhakt in the attribute-less sense, and at the same time he worshipped Ram as an incarnation.[16] Unlike Ramanuja, the saint Ramanand lived in the Bhakti period and his philosophy had an overriding influence on the movement, at least for the Vaishnava tradition. Besides, he is credited with having given a decisive push to the Bhakti movement in north India.

The academic world has been rife with contending theories on the 'Islam factor' in the explosion of the Bhakti movement. This is understandable given that the peak of the 'revolution', as various Indian and foreign experts have called it, virtually coincided with the establishment of the Mughal era, and both Bhakti and the Muslim rule continued for the next three centuries or so. Acharya Ramchandra Shukla and Hariprasad Dwivedi take opposite views on the issue of whether this Bhakti was a response to the growing Islamic influence. Dwivedi was dismissive. 'It is being said that when atrocities by the Muslims grew, the Hindu population took to singing devotional songs. It is ridiculous that when the Muslim rulers were destroying temples in north India, Hindu devotees would be seeking refuge in their gods in the south. Had Muslim cruelties been the cause of Bhakti, then that devotion ought to have been a movement in the Sindh, then in north India. Instead, it was most prevalent in the south.'[17] Dwivedi added that the Bhakti trend had begun centuries ago and had peaked during the Muslim rule; it was not a sudden flash of lightning which happened as being causal to Islam.

---

[15]*Hindi Sahitya: Udbhav aur Vikas*, Hazariprasad Dwivedi, 1952
[16]ibid
[17]ibid

But Shukla was convinced that the Bhakti movement gained momentum due to the anger over and fear of Muslim domination. 'The Hindus saw their temples being demolished, their deities crushed, and their icons humiliated. Frustrated and despairing of their impotence at being unable to stop any of these atrocities, what other way was left for the Hindus but to appeal to their gods to come to their rescue?'[18] He quotes Tulsidas in this context as saying that people who had come into India and ridiculed the Hindu faith needed to be tackled with strong measures.[19] He maintained that one of the chief reasons why the Bhakti movement spread to the north with speed was the growing cruelties on the Hindu community by the Muslim rulers.

He was to be repudiated. In his book, *Acharya Shukla aur Hindi Aalochana*, Ramvilas Sharma said that 'those who are seeking to establish a connection between the Hindu-Muslim confrontation and the hope-and-despair mood of medieval India, are unable to grasp the literary and social base of that time.'[20] Author and academician Meenakshi Jain too rejects the linkage, but for a different reason: 'The Bhakti movement has often been presented as a Hindu response to the egalitarian message of Islam and its spread among the lower classes. But this seems to be an inadequate assessment, as in the Hindu scheme Bhakti (devotion) is an essential constituent of sadhana (religious pursuit). It was mentioned in the Svetasvatara Upanishad as well as the *Bhagavad Gita*, where Lord Krishna said even the humblest

---

[18]*Hindi Sahitya ka Itihaas*; Acharya Ramachandra Shukla; Prakashan Sansthan, 2016
[19]ibid. '*Gorakh jagayo jog, Bhakti bhagayo log.*'
[20]*Paanch Bhakt Kavi: Vivad aur Vimarsh ke Sandarbh Mein*; Murli Manohar Prasad Singh; Bharatiya Jnanpith, 2017

devotee could reach him through simple devotion.'[21] It must be noted that Jain does not refer to the 'threat' of spreading Islam as the cause, or one of the primary causes, for the Bhakti revolution, but focuses on contesting the egalitarian argument.

The debate is here to stay because various reasons are being dug out and offered as credible explanations for the growth of the Bhakti trend. Some of the arguments drip with Marxist jugglery, even as they grudgingly admit to the Muslim influence. A research paper available on the Internet has this to state: 'The coming of Islam brought a new change in the social set-up of the country. The Muslim rulers adopted the policy of converting the Hindus to Islam. This, in turn, made the Hindus strengthen their hold, and the rule of the caste system was also tightened. In addition to this, rituals in the name of worship also increased majorly, on the part of the Hindus. All this change in the social custom led to another kind of reaction—the lower caste Hindus were tired of this rigid caste system, where they had to suffer the highest. The philosophy of Islam i.e. belief in one god and not following too many rituals in their mode of worship attracted the people of the lower strata to their faith.'[22] Presumably, this led to the Bhakti movement, which was monotheistic and egalitarian.

There are too many holes in this theory. One, Islam is not without rituals either. Two, no Bhakti poet asked people of the Hindu faith to abandon their religion; on the contrary, they promoted greater devotion to Hindu gods. And three, there is no empirical evidence to suggest that Bhakti poets appealed to either dualists or monists of the Hindu tradition not to embrace Islam. In fact, if we take Sufism, which is

---

[21]*A Storm of Songs*, John Stratton Hawley, 2015
[22]shodhganga.inflibnet.ac.in

considered an aspect of the Bhakti movement, the appeal is quite different: One of humanity and universalism and belief in that one higher entity.

Wendy Doniger too believes that Hinduism (in the present context, the Bhakti movement) came to little harm during the Mughal period; in fact, it made gains. 'Hinduisms of various kinds flourished under the Mughals.'[23] One reason was that, faced with a foreign religion, Islam, Hindu intellectuals took greater pains to preserve and promote the Hindu faith. The fact that the Bhakti phenomenon rose, grew and gained widespread acceptance during the Mughal rule, provides evidence for this line of thought. However, there can be the counter-argument that the fear of Islamic dominance, based on lived experience and not just imagination, fortified the movement. Also, to say that Hinduism prospered under the Mughals would be a sweeping statement. This may have been the case during Akbar's reign and to a lesser extent in the time of Jehangir and Shah Jahan, but it was certainly not true of Babur's and Aurangzeb's domination.

Author and politician Shashi Tharoor admits that 'Islam was initially a threat, and the attacks of Muslim invaders on temples and Hindu treasures, as well as the rape and abduction of Hindu women... led to a defensive closing of the ranks...'[24] But he also adds that once the Mughals settled down, 'Islamic percepts also played a part in the reshaping of Hinduism.'[25] The Muslim angle is reiterated elsewhere too: ' [The] Hindu community of India became much more conscious of its identity as a community under the stimulus of its contacts with the

---

[23]*The Hindus: An Alternative History*, Wendy Doniger, 2009
[24]*Why I Am a Hindu*; Shashi Tharoor; Aleph Book Company, 2018
[25]ibid

Islam of the Turks, Afghans and Muslims who invaded Indian in the medieval period.'[26]

The deeper we go into the socio-political world, the more we run the risk of missing out on the essentials: The charm and the innocence of Bhakti poetry and the unremitting faith of the poets in their gods, whether formed or formless. The clinical approach may have the cloak of academic respectability but it can turn into an impersonal and reductionist attempt at understanding what essentially is a very personal bonding between man and god. Mirabai cannot become a Marxist construct of a bourgeoisie-turned-proletariat; Ravidas cannot be viewed in simplistic terms as an oppressed lower caste who communicated with god much as he would with a slayer of the upper castes; Tulsidas cannot be branded as a hagiographer who was blind to the 'gender injustice' his hero, Lord Ram, supposedly committed on his wife. The Bhakti movement can be studied in different ways, but the core of the poetic movement advanced the roots of Hinduism deeper down in society. Indeed, the Bhakti revolution was the first demonstration of mass movement in favour of the Hindu faith.

That the Bhakti movement began from the south and spread across the country is well established. The Vaishnavite Alvar poets, of whom Nammalvar and Antal are most prominent, came from Tamil Nadu. Namdev and Tukaram were from Maharashtra; Narsi Mehta, from Gujarat; Nanak, Tulsidas, Surdas, Kabir and Mirabai based their activities in the northern parts of India; and Chaitanya 'Maha Prabhu' was a well-known Bhakti saint from the east. Arguably, Antal was the first female Bhakti poet, and she is said to have had miraculous powers.

---

[26]*Bhakti Religion in North India: Community Identity and Political Action*; Edited by David N. Lorenzen; SUNY Press, 1995

Born into a Brahmin family, 'legend has it that she came to be regarded as a reincarnation of Vishnu's wife Sri, and legend has it that she was absorbed into Vishnu's icon in the famous Vaishnava temple of Srirangam.'[27] The songs of the Alvar poets had a profound impact that was not limited to the south. 'The weeping, dancing and singing of the devotee, possessed by god, is characteristic of emotional devotionalism, the devotion of longing (Viraha Bhakti), so characteristic of the Alvars and later devotees of Krishna-Gopala.'[28] And, while the Vaishnavite order gained momentum in the Bhakti movement with Krishna as the focus, the cult of Rama too came to be popularized. That he was a Vaishnav icon helped, of course, but he came into his own during the medieval period. The credit for the Rama cult must go to Ramanand, who promoted devotion to Rama and Sita in a 'pure' sense—in contrast to the devotional style associated with Krishna and Radha, where mischief, romance and even eroticism were permitted.[29] The elevation of Krishna and Ram through the Bhakti revolution is a landmark in the journey of Hinduism, for they were to become the rallying points for religious-political movements in later years.

THE ENIGMATIC KABIR

Of the Bhakti poets, Kabir has remained the most enigmatic. Scholars have analyzed his writings in microscopic detail, and some have even devoted entire books to his study. Yet he remains elusive on both the personal and written front. Was he a Hindu or a Muslim? Was he a believer or a non-believer? Was his

---

[27] *An Introduction to Hinduism*, Gavin Flood, 2004
[28] ibid
[29] ibid

poetry metaphysical or emotional? In fact, does he even fit into the conventional definition of Bhakti? He was certainly a rebel and used sarcasm and wit to expose middlemen and power-brokers of religion. When he wrote, '*Ek achambha dekha re bhai…*'[30] he was sending across the powerful message of a misplaced understanding of religion. He was irreverent when he went on to state further in this poem that the strangeness he witnessed was that a lion was herding a cow; that the son came before the mother; that the teacher was paying obeisance to the student; that a fish was giving birth on a treetop; that the cat hunted the dog… and so on.

To say that Kabir rejected god, however, would be a wrong reading of his work. Whom was he referring to, if not god, when he wrote: '*Main ghulam mujhe bech Gosain/Tan-man-dhan mere Rajik tain…*'[31] meaning 'I am your servant, Ram (for Gosain is how the deity is referred to). I surrender my body, mind and material good to you.' His god, though, did not have attributes or form. On the other hand, he was unsparing of the religious leaders who went about preaching without following the tenets:[32]

> 'O Pandit! You go about your ways cleverly, having read the
> Shastras, and talk of mukti,
> What experiences have you yourself had of this mukti?
> You tell people that mukti is immersing one in the Supreme
> Being
> Where does that Supreme Being live? And what is his name?'

His attacks in this direction were unrelenting, and they encompassed both the Hindu and the Muslim religions. Perhaps

---

[30]*Paanch Bhakt Kavi*, Murli Manohar Prasad Singh, 2017
[31]ibid
[32]ibid. Translation is mine.

his most famous lines that reflected his philosophy of inner truth are the following: '*Mohe kahan dhoonere bandhu, main toh tere pass re / Na main deval na main masjid, na kaabe kailas main… Kahe Kabir sun bhai sadhu, sab swaanson ki swaans main* (Where do you look for me, friend/I am inside you/Not in the temple, not in the mosque, neither in Kaaba or Kailash/ Says Kabir, I am in every breath).'

John Stratton Hawley is right when he observes that Kabir, 'more than any other figure identified with the Bhakti movement seems to speak without mediation to modern sensibilities, and a good case can be made for freeing him from the historiographical ties that might otherwise bind him to the earlier reaches of medieval-ness.'[33] Using a different literary medium—that of the performative worlds in north India— writer Linda Hess[34] talks of the difficulty of understanding Kabir through the body of texts that are his own, and those which are *supposed* to have been his. 'Can we even gesture towards the real Kabir? Can we make any limiting statements about what he is likely to have said? Can the earliest dated manuscripts provide clue to Kabir's original utterances?' And yet, in the midst of these complexities, Kabir used everyday terms and telling analogies to express his message: The clay- and-potter, the blanket, the agricultural fields, and many more. For a Bhakti poet, he could be sometimes blunt, but even in that he would express the inevitability of things philosophically. Here is an instance of a grief-stricken widow accosting Kabir, and the poet's response:

---

[33]*A Storm of Songs*, John Stratton Hawley, 2015
[34]*Bodies of Song: Kabir Oral Traditions and Performative Worlds in North India;* Linda Hess; Permanent Black; First Indian printing in 2015 by permission of Oxford University Press

'The woman sobbed and cried:
We were joined, and now we are broken!
Kabir says, listen seekers
The one who joins
Is the one who breaks .'[35]

Given that Kabir espoused the rejection of Vedic rituals, ridiculed the Pandits and refused to be chained to the Hindu (or any) religious identity, how is he regarded as the foremost Bhakti poet? And in what way did he contribute to the promotion of Hindu faith? The answer to the first question has been given in the preceding lines. With regard to the second, it is to the credit of Hinduism—its famed flexibility and willingness to accommodate conflicting opinions—that it made use of Kabir's philosophy to cleanse (or attempt to cleanse) itself of the unwanted stuff. Hinduism's accommodating nature was evident also by the fact that Kabir flourished in Varanasi, the cradle of Hindu faith. The majority religion of the subcontinent thereafter acquired a more pronounced reformist touch.

SURDAS' DEVOTION

If Kabir was the nirgun, maverick poet of the Bhakti era, Surdas's poetry was suffused with devotion and trust for his personal god. His depiction of the many aspects of Krishna—the playful child, the flirtatious adolescent, the philosophical mentor, the realist, the divine reincarnation—was of the highest literary quality, and had a 'feel' which can come only with the unification of a human with his god. Prominent Hindi writer Baldev Vanshi called him the 'Poet of Poets'.[36] Surdas, more than any other Vaishnav poet of

---

[35]ibid

[36]*Mahakavi Surdas*; Edited by Baldev Vanshi; Prakashan Sansthan, 2013

the Bhakti period, contributed to the lore of Krishna and placed the deity firmly on the map of the pantheon of Hindu gods and goddesses. The wave of love-devotion which he generated in north India continues to provide succour to troubled and grief-stricken devotees to this day.[37] For John Stratton Hawley, Surdas was an ideal poet,[38] dedicated to his Lord and his singing, and yet never seeming to abandon a sense of personal struggle, both material and spiritual, which came from his impoverished family background. In popular narrative, Surdas was visually impaired, and this only strengthened his reputation of having a spiritual vision that allowed him to see and understand things that the sighted could not. With the evils of the world literally out of his sight, he could shape his poetry from unadulterated love. In his book,[39] Hawley conducts a little study of his own on the subject by picking a few of Surdas's lines, and it would be worthwhile to dwell on those observations in passing.

'Lord, you know with an inward knowing,
All of the deeds I've done,
How blind, how base, how blank I've been
Yet you've counted my counterfeit as right.'

There should be no doubt here that the use of 'blind' ('andh' is the Hindi word Surdas uses) is not related to a physical condition but refers to moral failings. A more compelling case of the opposite is, however, made out in the following lines addressed to Ram (one of the references to Krishna; the poet switches between Ram and Krishna as being one):

'They say you're so self-giving, self-denying, Ram,

---

[37]ibid
[38]*Surdas: Poet, Singer, Saint*; John Stratton Hawley; Primus Books, 2018
[39]ibid

That you offered Sudama the four goals of life
And to your guru you granted a son.
Vibhishan: you gave him the land of Lanka
To honour his early devotion to you.

Ravan: his were the ten heads you severed,
Simply by reaching for your bow.
Prahlad: you justified the claim he made.
Indra: leader of the gods, you made a sage.
Surdas: how could you be so harsh with him—
Leaving him without his very eyes?'

His blindness can be a subject of debate, but what is irrefutably established is Surdas's preeminent position in Bhakti poetry. He was a master at expressing the sentiment of viraha (separation from a loved one) and the resultant longing. This could be a longing for a fellow human or for god. There were times when Surdas felt he was weakening in his devotion because of distractions, and then would cry out:

'I am pleading with you to turn, hear this wretch,
Who dies to sing your praises.
That mistral Maya has got out her stick,
And put me through a monkey's paces:
Door to door she's goaded me to dance,
In every sort of skit and show…
Surdas says, if you have no mercy,
Who else can make me forget my pain?'

His intense devotional style, innocence and the sense of surrender to god endeared him to millions in the northern belt of India and played a monumental role in drawing and retaining vast swathes of the population to the Hindu faith, at a time when the pulls of external challenges and internal upheavals between traditionalists and reformists had taken serious proportions.

One of the prominent reformers of the Bhakti era was Ravidas. Born to an underprivileged class, he expressed his sense of frustration and sorrow without mincing words, and appealed to god in a direct fashion. At times, he used irony to convey his message:[40]

'You and me, me and you: what difference does it make?
It's like gold and a golden bracelet, water and wave.
You who have no limits, if I didn't sin
How could they call you Redeemer of Fallen Men?'

Ravidas may not have been studied as much as the other poets of the Bhakti tradition, but like Kabir, he created the space for dissent without violent defiance and presented social inequities as man-made and not god-given. As we have seen above, he appealed to the almighty to pull him out of his misery. There is some variation in opinion on whether Ravidas believed in a god with attributes, or that without. Many modern-day scholars hold the latter to be true, though Ravidas himself was ambivalent in his poems. Take this, for example, where the 'Lord' remains undefined and unnamed:

'Ravidas says, what shall I sing?
Singing, singing I am defeated.
How long shall I consider and proclaim:
Absorb the self into the Self.

This experience is such,
That it defies all description.
I have met the Lord,
Who can cause me harm?'[41]

---

[40]*A Storm of Songs*, John Stratton Hawley, 2015
[41]*Indian Religions: A Historical Reader of Spiritual Expression and Experience*; Edited

THE 'SURRENDERED' ONES

Other poets of the time, especially Mirabai and Tulsidas, made enormous contributions—which have become embedded in the collective Hindu psyche—through their magical poetry. Mirabai was not just a rebel but, to use modern-day terminology, a sort of feminist, when she spurned her husband and family in favour of god, and declared: '*Mere toh Girdhar Gopal / Doosro na koi* (Krishna alone is mine, none else).' There are many populist and hagiographic accounts of Mirabai, such as Krishna coming to her rescue when she was sought to be poisoned by her in-laws or when she was set up to be bitten by a snake. The poison failed to work and the snake turned into an idol of her personal god.[42] These fantastic stories apart, it is indisputable that Mirabai's unquestioned devotion to the deity Krishna and the charming lyrical quality of her songs not only established her as among the Bhakti movement's most significant poets, but also greatly expanded the Vaishnavite tradition, which began from the south, in north India. With her message of freedom and her determination to counter social obstacles that came her way, she must have secretly—given those days—gladdened the hearts of many Indian women who were compelled to remain subordinate to an oppressively feudal and patriarchal system. Mirabai wasn't the queen of Jhansi, to take on a sword and ride into the battlefield; she won through the message of love and devotion. English language writers have been suitably influenced by her poetry and have laboured to decipher many meanings in them—ranging from Bhakti to feminism to a crusader against social injustice, etc. But unalloyed devotion

---

by Peter Heehs; NYU Press, 2002
[42]*Mira Bai*; Usha Nilsson; Sahitya Akademi, 1997

to god has remained at the core. Her popularity, even today, is perhaps higher than other Bhakti poets—films have been made on her in both the southern and the northern languages, and her bhajans are commonly heard on various occasions. Her poetry had both compassion and the pain of longing for her beloved Krishna, which turned her into a heartthrob for generations. Here is a sample,[43] though it must be said that it fails to capture the beauty of the original lines—not because the translation is faulty, but that it's impossible to do justice to Mirabai's magical lyrics in the original:

'My Dark One has gone to an alien land.
He has left me behind, he's never returned, he's never sent me a single word.
So I've stripped off my ornaments, jewels and adornments, cut my hair from my head.
And put on holy garments, all on his account, seeking him in all four directions,
Mira: unless she meets the Dark One, her Lord, she doesn't even want to live.'

As for Tulsidas, his *Ram Charit Manas* (composed in the Awadhi dialect) changed the face of Ram Bhakti for good. Until his magnum opus came along, there was only the Ramayana in Sanskrit, which was out of reach for millions of readers. He spent most of his time in Varanasi composing his epic, and is said to have founded the famous Sankat Mochan temple in that ancient city. 'It can be said without reservation that Tulsidas is the greatest poet to write in the Hindi language.'[44] It is said that when challenged by a priest at a Krishna temple

---

[43]Translated by John Stratton Hawley.
[44]*Encyclopedia of Hinduism*; Edited by Constance A. Jones & James D. Ryan; Facts on File Inc, 2007

in Vrindavan, who said he who bows to any deity other than their Ishta Devata is a fool, Tulsidas said:

> 'O Lord! How shall I describe today's splendour,
> for you appear auspicious
> Tulsidas will down his head when you take the bow and
> arrow in your hands.'

At this, the idol of Krishna holding a flute turned into an idol of Ram with a bow and arrow.

By the time the Bhakti movement era came to a close, it had finally achieved what earlier proponents of the religion had wished for but for various reasons could not fully realize—vociferously engage the common man from all walks of life and from all corners of the country to the Hindu faith. Meanwhile, three gentlemen, very different from one another in temperament and with separate areas of operation, but bound by a common commitment to Hinduism and associated spirituality, were preparing to take the national Hindu narrative by storm and have its reverberations heard across the oceans too. They were Narendranath Dutta, Bal Gangadhar Tilak and Aurobindo Ghosh. The first was an ascetic who transformed into the legendary Swami Vivekananda, the second a politician whom the British called the 'father of Indian unrest', and the third a revolutionary-turned-spiritual philosopher, revered as Sri Aurobindo. It was time for a mix of realpolitik and religious spiritualism.

FOUR

Now an Organization, then Mobilisation

The Vedanta recognises no sin, it only recognises error.
And the greatest error, says the Vedanta, is to say that
you are weak, that you are a sinner, a miserable creature,
and that you have no power and you cannot do this or that.

SWAMI VIVEKANANDA

For all the valiant efforts of past masters, poets and teachers, the journey of Hinduism would probably have sputtered and lost momentum, even if temporarily, but for the efforts of Swami Vivekananda, 'Lokmanya' Tilak and Sri Aurobindo. They worked in a particularly difficult time, when the British had cracked down hard on nationalists following the 1857 revolt—the First War of Independence, as many observers call it. Assertive elements, both in politics and the socio-religious sphere, were special targets of their attention. While Tilak and Aurobindo (in his early, revolutionary avatar) faced the British wrath, the Swami had it easier since he had steered clear of politics. And yet, the colonial rulers could not have been unaware of the campaign he had studiously constructed to unite people by the overarching spirituality of the Vedanta. If they didn't respond, it was probably because Swami Vivekananda's movement did not overtly challenge the imperial rule. Besides, he had become an international figure after his participation in the Parliament of Religions held in Chicago in September 1893, and picked up known figures as his disciples from Britain too. His hard-sell of Hinduism as a religion with universal values has become the bedrock of any analysis of his contributions, but what has not attracted the attention it deserved is what he did on his return to India: He sought to institutionalize the faith so that its message could be more effectively dispersed among the masses. But of course, he did not attempt to do it the Western way, by finding a papal authority. His idea of an institution was to set up mechanisms that would serve as the 'Organization'.[1]

He had quipped to one of his admirers that he had succumbed to a temptation during his visit to the United States. When asked playfully who that lucky girl was, he had laughingly said, 'Organization.' But his fellow monks were far from amused when he returned and laid before them his idea.[2] They wondered how the concepts of Bhakti and Mukti reconciled with the establishment of an organization and related social activities. Cut to the quick, the Swami retorted, 'You are Bhaktas... sentimental fools. You are only good at praying with folded hands: "O Lord! How beautiful is your nose, how sweet are your eyes," and all such nonsense.' He was so carried away that he even said a few harsh things about his teacher, Ramakrishna Paramhamsa. Later, though, he was remorseful about the outburst, but stuck to the idea of creating structures to promote the universal teachings of Hinduism, particularly the Vedantic ones. In his opinion, Bhakti alone is unidimensional, and goes against the Upanishad's core teaching of 'Neti, Neti' (It is not this alone, it is not this alone). He wanted to use

---

[1] *Swami Vivekanand: The Living Vedanta*; Chaturvedi Badrinath; Penguin Books India, 2006
[2] ibid

the organization to reach out to the masses. As he said in a letter[3] about his task: 'A hundred thousand men and women, fired with the zeal of holiness, fortified with eternal faith in the Lord and...lion's courage by their sympathy for the poor and the fallen and the downtrodden, will go over the length and breadth of the land, preaching the gospel of salvation, the gospel of help, the gospel of social raising-up—the gospel of equality.' In one brilliant stroke, thus, he presented Hinduism as a mass movement that spreads devotion, equality, and social upliftment. This is significant, as he 'lived before the era of mass politics.'[4] He was not the first, though, to understand the potency of an organization to take religion forward; Adi Shankaracharya, as we have seen earlier in the book, had established four principal 'mutts', each headed by successive Shankaracharyas, with a similar aim.

Swami Vivekananda has been construed by some contemporary era scholars as a spiritual leader who was more of a universal humanist than a proponent of Hinduism. Though the Swami's spiritualism was indeed humanistic, it would be silly to ignore the fact that he was driven to this task by his Hindu faith and his trust in the Upanishadic Vedanta. That he was quick to balance things out, does not take away from his contribution to the propagation of Hinduism.[5] His rallying call to 'bring all together'[6] was in keeping with the efforts of earlier teachers such as the Adi Shankaracharya and the Bhakti poets. This is the message he had conveyed at the Chicago conference, though he later remarked that he had not gone to

[3]ibid
[4]*Incarnations: India in 50 Lives*, Sunil Khilnani, 2016
[5]ibid
[6]ibid

the US with the purpose of delivering his famed lecture, nor was he enamoured by such functions, though he called it a 'great affair'.[7] But he also realized the need to 'internationalize' Hinduism and rid it of the misconceptions that the West had. In one of his letters,[8] Swami Vivekananda stated, 'You may not understand why a sanyasin should be in America. But it was necessary, because the only claim you have to be recognized by the world is your religion, and good specimens of our religious men are required to be sent abroad to give other nations an idea that India is not dead.'

VIVEKANANDA'S HINDUISM

What we referred to as 'balancing things out', Chaturvedi Badrinath calls 'simultaneity' in the Swami's life.[9] He revered the Buddha, but was critical of historical Buddhism. He antagonized a prominent monk during one of his lectures in the US, to the extent that the religious leader, from what is now Sri Lanka, felt compelled to write a letter to him in protest—a letter that dripped with malice.[10] At a lecture delivered in San Francisco in the US in March 1900,[11] Swami Vivekananda praised Buddhism as the 'most tremendous religious movement that the world ever saw.' He said he was very fond of Buddha, 'but not his doctrine.' In the course of his lecture referred to above, he stated, 'There was an element of danger in the teaching of the Buddha: it was a reforming religion. In order to bring about

---

[7]*Swami Vivekananda: The Living Vedanta*, Chaturvedi Badrinath, 2006
[8]ibid
[9]ibid
[10]ibid
[11]*Vivekananda: World Teacher*; Edited by Swami Adiswarananda; Rupa Publications India Pvt Ltd, 2007

the tremendous spiritual change he did, he had to give many negative teachings. But if a religion emphasizes the negative side too much, it is in danger of eventual destruction.'

But his simultaneity also encompassed Hinduism. For instance, he wrote, 'No religion on earth preaches the dignity of humanity in such a lofty strain as Hinduism, and no religion on earth treads upon the necks of the poor and low in such a fashion as Hinduism.'[12] But throughout, Swami Vivekananda did not let go of the 'gem' of Hinduism. In one of his reflections on the 'problem of modern India and its solutions', he observed: '…we must always keep the wealth of our own home before our eyes, so that everyone, down to the masses, may always know and see what his own ancestral property is. We must exert ourselves to do that; and side by side, we should be brave to open our doors to receive available light from outside.'[13] Hinduism, for him, was a journey that never ends. 'The idea of a Personal God, the Ruler and the Creator of this universe, as He has been styled, the Ruler of Maya, or nature, is not the end of these Vedantic ideas; it is only the beginning. The idea grows and grows until the Vedantist finds that He who, he thought, was standing outside, is he himself and is in reality within. He is the one who is free, but who through limitation thought he was bound.'[14] He believed that the journey of Hinduism is the journey of understanding our real self. At a speech in London, he said: 'So long as we have no knowledge of our real nature, we are beggars, jostled about by every force in nature and made slaves of by everything in nature. We cry all over the world, but help never comes. We cry to an imaginary being and yet

[12]*Incarnations: India in 50 Lives*, Sunil Khilnani, 2016
[13]*Reflections*, Swami Vivekananda, Om Books International, 2018
[14]ibid

it never comes. But still, we hope help will come; and thus in weeping, wailing, and hoping, this life is passed and the same play goes on and on.'[15]

Given his corpus of work and the broad range of thoughts, it becomes difficult to categorize Swami Vivekananda. Was he a Hindu Nationalist, or a Universalist teacher? He was certainly a proud Hindu who spread the religion's positive message far and wide in the country and on foreign land. He was also a nationalist because every time he addressed audiences, he kept India and its great cultural traditions in focus. And yet the dilemma of labelling him remains. No such problem needs to be associated with 'Lokmanya' Bal Gangadhar Tilak, who not just wore his religion unapologetically on his sleeves, but was also assertive about it. He was arguably the first 'Hindu Nationalist' politician of prominence and served as an effective counter, both in religious and political ways, to the 'other camp', which in his opinion sought to demean and render ineffective the majority faith. His battle was with people both within his Congress party and outside. Tilak was a great admirer of Swami Vivekananda and often drew inspiration from him. But, unlike Swami Vivekananda or Sri Aurobindo, Tilak did not view Hinduism from an intellectual or spiritual prism; instead, he saw it as a rallying force both against the British rule and the minority community. His Hinduism was crafted to serve the need of the hour—and that was freedom from imperial reign. The 'Swaraj is my birthright and I shall have it' slogan was the fulcrum of his politics, and his religion was one of the many elements he deployed towards that purpose. And because of his aggressive approach, he became the magnet for a number of freedom-fighters such as Bipin Chandra Pal and Lala Lajpat Rai,

---

[15]*Vivekananda: World Teacher*, Ed. Swami Adishwarananda, 2006

who held the view that mere constitutional means and pacifist conduct would not make the British leave the country. It was not long before he came to be considered one of the leading 'radicals' in the Congress, which incidentally then also included Aurobindo Ghose.[16]

The year when Swami Vivekananda delivered his famous Chicago address was also the year when Tilak converted the Ganeshotsav celebrations into a mass event. It was meant to demonstrate 'Hindu power' on a grand scale and send a message to both the British and the non-Hindu community—especially the Muslims—that the Hindus could not be taken for granted. Besides, he realized that this festival was celebrated by Hindus cutting across caste lines, and he found in it an opportunity to 'bridge the gap between the Brahmins and the non-Brahmins'.[17] This was also the period when public gatherings, whether social or political, had been banned by the British, who had yet to get over the alarm of the 1857 revolt. Perhaps he took a cue from Chhatrapati Shivaji, who had initiated a public display of Ganeshotsav during his rule. It is not coincidental that Tilak also popularized Shiv Jayanti to mark the birth anniversary of the Maratha king a year after he kicked off the public event on Ganesh Chaturthi. It is possible that Tilak was aware of his base in Maharashtra and thus chose these region-specific events to fortify his image. Also, given that Shivaji had a reputation for standing up to the Mughal rule, although he was not against Muslims per se, Tilak's politics gained from the association. Whatever may have been the case, he ended up with a legacy that continues to this day. At that point in time, he had stated:

---

[16]*The Nationalist Movement: Indian Political Thought from Ranade to Bhave*; Donald Mackenzie Brown; University of California Press, 1970
[17]indiatoday.in, September 5, 2016

'In every country and in every age a religious festival serves as an occasion for the display of the best output of knowledge and the intuition of the people in the matter of the fine and the aesthetic arts.'[18]

TILAK: A POLITICAL VOICE

As Tilak immersed himself in the burly world of politics, challenging the high and mighty in the Congress and ridiculing them for their 'moderation' in the face of grave challenges that faced the Hindu community and the nation at large, his family counselled him to take it easy. 'Tilak's mother-in-law murmured that he should now leave the dangerous field of politics and follow a calm and quiet life... Tilak respectfully replied that events were taking place according to the spirit of the times. Men's destinies were shaped by a higher power than by their inclinations or aptitudes.'[19] This philosophical response is interesting. Were Tilak's 'inclinations and aptitudes' different from the direction he had taken, or was he merely expressing a larger point? In any case, nothing seemed to stop the firebrand leader, not even health issues (he was by then suffering from serious knee pains, among other things). 'Tilak was now gradually shifting to what the Moderates called Extremism... The Congress was now nothing more than a lifeless body, a resort for lawyers and title-holders, who sought relaxation in it.'[20] This may not have been entirely true, for there were those in the party who had given up luxuries of life and plunged

---

[18]*Lokmanya Tilak: Father of the Indian Freedom Struggle*; Dhananjay Keer; Popular Prakashan, Third Edition, 2016
[19]ibid
[20]ibid

themselves into the freedom struggle, enduring the atrocities of the British. Nonetheless, there was some restiveness over the laxity of the Congress in effectively countering the socio-political situation—not to mention the communal divide.

Tilak's opponents were especially vehement in their criticism of the 'religion card' he had introduced in the freedom movement. 'It was their belief that religious awakening or reveal would torment hatred of others and in the end would be destructive to national unity... Tilak's reply to them was that there was no example in history in which national solidarity or national prosperity became a certainty because religion was destroyed and people became religion-less.'[21] He was convinced that Hindus could be united through a 'religious awakening without creating a sense of hatred or opposition to other religionists.' He firmly believed in the force of Hinduism as a unifying factor in the fight against oppressive rule. It is fashionable to say today that Tilak's belligerent conduct put him in a minority in the Congress, but that was far from true. At least in Maharashtra, his opinions counted. Senior leaders of the Congress privately requested Tilak to refrain from attacking the Congress since it was leading to drying out of funds for the party from the State. Dhananjay Keer quotes from a correspondence Dadabhai Naorojee had with Tilak, in which he said that Tilak would only 'weaken and discourage the only body (Congress) through whom India has to work out its redemption.'[22]

But Tilak was not to be deterred, because he staunchly believed that far from weakening the Congress, he was strengthening the party by seeking its focus on what he considered to be the right and relevant issues—the power of the Hindu community,

---

[21]ibid
[22]ibid

and the imperative to tap it, being chief among them. While his campaign fetched him several admirers across the western and northern parts of India, the south had remained relatively less infected by the nationalist zeal. But there was an exception. One young man by the name of Chidambaram Pillai, from what is now Tamil Nadu, was deeply impressed by Tilak's zeal, so much so that he did the unthinkable: He launched a shipping firm to take on the British Steam Navigation Company, which had a fleet of over a hundred ships,[23] and provocatively named it the Swadeshi Steam Navigation Company. The Swadeshi firm began to eat into the British company's business, leading the latter to constantly lower its tariff.[24] In fact, the British firm resorted to trickery to lure customers. It 'offered promotions like free umbrellas, and hung a board using the word 'Swadeshi' to confuse Indians into buying tickets for the wrong line.'[25] By the time Pillai had the chance to meet Tilak, the divide between the 'extremists' and the 'moderates' had deepened. Tilak handed over the charge of his faction in the south to him. The Pillai episode must have gladdened Tilak's heart, though the thought may or may not have crossed his mind that it was perhaps the first instance of a Swadeshi movement, which would in later years be given a new thrust by Mahatma Gandhi.

Unlike Swami Vivekananda or Sri Aurobindo, Tilak was not an authority on Hinduism. But while he adroitly grasped the political significance of mobilizing the Hindu community and concentrated his attention on this aspect, he also studied texts such as the *Bhagavad Gita* and offered interpretations on Karma Yoga that have become quite popular—*Shrimad Bhagavad*

---

[23]*Incarnations: India in 50 Lives*, Sunil Khilnani, 2016
[24]ibid
[25]ibid

Gita Rahasya being one of them. He even tried to date the Vedas by interpreting the positions of various stars (nakshatras) described in the sacred texts. In his commentaries on the Gita, he emphasized the need for activism, which the sacred book spoke of, and juxtaposed it in the present context, also falling back on Ramanuja's analysis of the book.[26] It is said by some critics that his oft-quoted examples from the Hindu texts irritated the Muslim community members, who suspected that he was seeking to present India as a Hindu nation, and this may have led many of them to veer towards the British.

Incidentally, Tilak is often presented as a conservative who opposed reforms among the Hindu community. For instance, he was personally not in favour of child marriage, but he opposed moves by the British to clamp down on the practice on the ground that they were seeking to interfere in Hindu affairs. He is also said to have frowned upon the idea of Hindu women working and believed they needed to be at home and take care of the family.[27] The counter-argument is that Tilak took such positions because he apprehended that the struggle for freedom from foreign yoke would be subsumed in the zeal for social reforms. 'In private conversation Tilak often expressed [thoughts] to his friends concurrent in the views of the reformers. But his friends were surprised to hear Tilak opposing the reformers in public. When once he privately endorsed the views of the reformers, his daughter asked why Dada (that's how his children dressed him) then opposed the reformers. He replied that he was not prepared

---

[26]'The Secular as Sacred?—The Religio-political Rationalization of B. G. Tilak'; Mark Harvey; *Modern Asian Studies* 20(2); Cambridge University Press, 1986

[27]*Makers of Modern India*, Ramachandra Guha, 2011

to go into the wilderness!'[28] This may have been said in jest, but it demonstrated the leader's shrewdness in realising that following the herd does not a leader make. He had his image to take care of—an image which was essential to sustain the Hindu feelings of identity and nationalism. Whatever the case may have been, these instances only served to strengthen his image of a non-reformist, though they did little to reduce his reputation of a no-nonsense leader of the kind that the country, and the Congress in particular, needed. The focus on Tilak has been on his anti-reform stance, and little attention is paid to his valiant struggles for the upliftment of farmers. This was a reformist drive. He protested loud and strong against the various laws and rules that governed the taxation of farmers. At a time when many leaders refused to speak up for the country's toiling masses for fear of antagonizing the British, Tilak's own articles bore the title, 'Will the Peasants Have to Revolt?' Pointing out that the people were burdened with taxes, that the population was increasing and trade was declining, and that the government was becoming costlier and land growing less fertile, he emphatically remarked that these factors presented a very horrible picture, and it was not impossible that there would be a revolt.[29]

Even in pursuance of his Hindu credentials, Tilak was pragmatic. When leaders of the Christian and the Muslim communities appealed for brotherhood with the majority religion, he pointed out that 'it would happen when all other people also behaved well towards the Hindus.'[30] He added that the British sided with the Muslims not because they loved the community, but to divide Indians and perpetuate their rule.

---

[28]*Lokmanya Tilak*, Dhananjay Keer, Third Edition, 2016
[29]ibid
[30]ibid

He claimed that the British were afraid of the Hindu majority which was gradually awakening; the Muslims, on the other hand, were apprehensive that they were being left behind in areas of development. But Tilak wasn't going to lose sleep over these matters. His efforts at creating a Hindu identity in the process led to the discontinuation of Hindu participation in Muharram. 'The Hindus, who had been so far participating in the Muharram celebrations, now gave it up. He harnessed their energy in organizing the Ganesh festival, and thus people got a substitute.'[31] Whether they were looking for a substitute is beside the point, but the truth is that Tilak crafted for himself an image of a non-compromiser. He was not a militant in the strict sense of the term, but he wasn't going to shun militant revolutionaries who were ready to sacrifice their lives for the country's freedom. 'He often said that he would join a revolt provided there was any possibility of success.'[32]

SRI AUROBINDO: THE INTELLECTUAL

Aurobindo Ghose had a little of both Tilak and Swami Vivekananda in him. The zeal to stand up and wield the stick if necessary and dispose of political correctness were qualities Tilak displayed. His search for a larger truth—and in the process dispel the darkness of ignorance by lighting the candle of Hinduism, as a transformed Sri Aurobindo—matched the intellectual rigour of Swami Vivekananda. While the philosophical directions the two spiritual leaders took were different, they approximated in the essence. Sri Aurobindo's contribution to the promotion of

---

[31]ibid. Keer erroneously uses the term 'celebration' for Muharram, which is a sober event 'observed', not celebrated.
[32]ibid

Hindu religion and spirituality was both original and robust. Although as an intellectual he was willing to absorb critical observations about Hinduism, he would not take unfounded or misinterpreted condemnation lying down, hitting back with intellectual vehemence. Responding to William Archer's critique[33] of the Hindu faith, he said: 'When he (Archer) denies that there is any real morality in Hinduism or affirms that it has never claimed morale teaching as one of its functions, statements that are the exact contrary of the facts, when he goes so far as to say Hinduism is the character of the people and it indicates a melancholy proclivity towards whatever is monstrous and unwholesome, one can only conclude that truth-speaking is not one of the ethical virtues which Mr Archer though it necessary to practice or at least that it need be no part of a rationalist's criticism of religion.'[34] Trashing the argument presented by certain intellectuals, that too much indulgence in religion by the country's majority population had been the nation's undoing, he stated, 'If the majority of Indians had indeed made the whole of their lives religion in the true sense of the word, we should not be where we are now; it was because their public life became most irreligious, egoistic, self-seeking, materialistic that they fell.'[35]

He was arguably talking in the context of all religions that thrived in India, but his other writings clearly indicated that he was more preoccupied with the Hindu faith. His thoughts on the *Bhagavad Gita* are not just illuminating but present the sacred text in a larger context that ought to not be bound within the

---

[33]William Archer was essentially a dramatist who wrote a critical commentary titled, 'India and the Future', in 1917.

[34]'The Renaissance in India—A Defence of India Culture'; *The Complete Works of Sri Aurobindo*; Volume 20; Sri Aurobindo Ashram, 1997

[35]ibid

confines of one particular religion. His observations are even more relevant in the present context, when the glorification of books such as the Gita is seen as the promotion of a Hindu India. 'In the Gita there is very little that is merely local or temporal and its spirit is so large, profound and universal that even this little can easily be universalized without the sense of the teaching suffering any diminution or violation; rather by giving an ampler scope to it than belonged to the country and epoch, the teaching gains in depth, truth and power.'[36] Contextualizing the sacred text, he added, 'The Gita is not a weapon for dialectical warfare; it is a gate opening on the whole world of spiritual truth and experience and the view it gives us embraces all the provinces of that supreme region. It maps out, but it does not cut up or build walls or hedges to confine our vision.'[37]

The Vedas have for long been the target of attacks by those who believe that this corpus of compositions is primarily responsible for the ills in Hinduism. Negations of the Hindu faith have come largely in opposition to the Vedic literature. 'Secular' authors and commentators have made the Vedas a special target of their incessant assaults, in the hope perhaps that, if they can discredit that which is the most ancient Hindu text and on whose foundation the Hindu faith has progressed, they will have achieved 50 per cent of their task. They also seized on the Vedantist movement erroneously as a rejection of the Vedic culture, forgetting in their enthusiasm that the Vedantists themselves had not dismissed outright the Vedas as noxious, but only sought to frame a fresh narrative. 'From the historical point of view the Rig Veda may be regarded as a record of the great advance made by humanity by special means at a certain period

---

[36]'Essays on the Gita', *The Complete Works of Sri Aurobindo*, Volume 19, 1998
[37]ibid

of its collective progress. In its esoteric, as well as its exoteric significance, it is the Book of Works, on the inner and outer sacrifice, it is the spirit...of battle and victory as it discovers and climbs to planes of thought and experience inaccessible to the natural or animal man, man's praise of the divine Light, Power and Grace at work in the mortal.'[38] Sri Aurobindo went a step further and said that the 'Vedic Word was a seed of thought and vision by which they (sages of the Upanishads) recovered old truths in new forms.'[39] But he did accept that the Vedantic movement led to the 'disintegration of the old Vedic thought and culture',[40] though, even here, it must be observed that this was a welcome switch not of outright rejection of the old but of acceptance of a new order. He made an interesting distinction with the following: 'The Veda for the priests, the Vedanta for the sages.'[41] That Sri Aurobindo wasn't inclined to trash the Vedas is evident from his various writings on the subject, such as *Vedic and Philological Studies* and *Hymns to the Mystic Fire* (which is a translation of the Vedic hymns to Agni from the Rig Veda). From essays on the *Bhagavad Gita* to the Vedas, and to the Upanishads,[42] Sri Aurobindo went deeper and deeper into understanding the essence of the ancient texts, and concluded that they offered both spiritual light and knowledge.

His analysis was critical, given that Western scholars, according to him, often erred in grasping the core and ended up displaying the superficial. He was scathing in his observation

---

[38]'The Secret of the Veda', *The Complete Works of Sri Aurobindo*, Volume 15, 1998
[39]ibid
[40]ibid
[41]ibid
[42]Upanishad I: 'Isha Upanishad', *The Complete Works of Sri Aurobindo*, Volume 17, 2003; Upanishad II: 'Kena and Other Upanishads', *The Complete Works of Sri Aurobindo*, Volume 18, 2001

of the poor quality of interpretation by European academics. 'It is certainly not creditable to European scholarship that after so many decades of Sanskrit research, the problem of the Mahabharata which should be the pivot for all the rest, has remained practically untouched. For it is not an exaggeration to say that European scholarship has shed no light whatever on the Mahabharata beyond the bare fact, that is the work of more than one hand. All else it has advanced, and fortunately (emphasis mine) it has advanced little, has been rash, arbitrary or prejudiced; theories, theories, always theories without any honestly industrious consideration of the problem.'[43] There is yet another comment he throws at the European mind with the force of a hundred missiles all let loose at once, and which should give food for thought to certain present-day academics: 'For, to the European, Sanskrit words are no more than dead counters which he can play with and show as he likes into places the most unnatural or combinations the most monstrous; to the Hindus they are living things…whose temperament he understands and whose possibilities he can judge to a hair.'[44] He then added a bit that is eerily similar to the sorry state of affairs in the present day, 'That with these advantages (of having the right temperament) Indian scholars have not been able to form themselves into a great and independent school of learning, is due to two causes: The miserable scantiness of the mastery in Sanskrit provided by our universities, crippling to all but born scholars, and our lack of a sturdy independence which makes us over-ready to defer to European authority.'[45] But he ended on the positive note that these failings were easily surmountable.

---

[43]'Early Cultural Writings', *The Complete Works of Sri Aurobindo*, Volume 1, 2003
[44]ibid
[45]ibid

Interestingly a similar refrain—of Indian scholars not being able to counter Western narratives—has also been in recent years made by the likes of Rajiv Malhotra.[46] Shrinivas Tilak suggests: 'A major challenge for Hindu researchers is to retrieve sufficient space to convince the various fragmented but powerful research communities (Western and Hindu/Indian in the diaspora or in India) of the need for greater Hindu involvement in research on Hinduism. Yet another challenge is to develop approaches toward research that take into account, without being limited by, the legacies of previous Western-Dominated research and the parameters of both previous and current approaches.'[47]

It is a reflection on Sri Aurobindo's titanic contribution that his writings on spiritualism and Hindu scriptures and sacred books have been a subject of debate and dissertations across the world. Part of this must no doubt have been triggered by the desire of Western scholars to prove wrong his views about their inadequacies. There are, though, books which undertake a serious understanding of the teacher's profundity and the 'applicability of his ideas on Indian culture and polity.'[48] Whatever the reasons may be behind the surge of interest among foreigner writers, the cause of Hinduism in India, coupled with the faith's spiritual content, has received a smart boost.

As a revolutionary freedom-fighter, before he abandoned that path and relocated to Pondicherry to begin a new innings as the great spiritual guru, Aurobindo did not fuse his Hindu identity with that of politics of the day, unlike Tilak. But

---

[46]Rajiv Malhotra is an author and commentator, who has taken on Western Indologists such as Sheldon Pollock and Wendy Doniger.
[47]*Situating Sri Aurobindo: A Reader*; Edited by Peter Heehs; Oxford University Press, 2013
[48]*The Life of Hinduism*; Edited by John Stratton Hawley & Vasudha Narayanan; Aleph Book Company, 2017

he admired Tilak and even endorsed him for taking on the 'moderates' and being politically incorrect when circumstances so warranted. And he was merciless in taking on those who aligned themselves against Tilak on the pretext that the latter was an 'extremist' and lacked tact. Writing in August 1906, at a time when Tilak was facing a barrage of attacks on his brand of politics—which was supposedly a good criterion to deny him the Congress president's post—Sri Aurobindo said in response to comments by *The Indian Mirror* (a publication sympathetic to the 'moderates' within the party): 'It is not, apparently, the acknowledged leader of one of the greatest Indian races who can aspire to that post; it is a man of "tact"—one, in other words, who does not like to offend the authorities. It is not the great protagonist and champion of Swadeshi in western India; it is a man of moderate views: one, let us say, who dare not look Truth in the face and speak out boldly what he thinks. It is not the man whom the whole Hindu community in western India delights to honour, from Peshawar to Kolhapur and from Bombay to our own borders; it is one who will not talk about Shivaji and Bhavani—only about Mahatmas. It is not the man who has suffered and denied himself for his country's welfare and never abased his courage nor bowed his head under the most crushing persecution; it is the one who by refusing to honour similar course in others, dishonours the country for which they have suffered.'[49] Aurobindo then continued in his unsparing fashion to state: 'Mr Tilak's only offence is the course and boldness of his views and his sturdiness in holding by them. He has dared to go to jail and honour those who follow his example—the bold bad man!'[50]

---

[49]'Bande Mataram', *The Complete Works of Sri Aurobindo*, Volumes 6 & 7, 2002
[50]ibid

Aurobindo's praise for Tilak was fulsome, and it often came at the cost of the Lokmanya's ideological opponents within the Congress. Disparaging in his opinion on a piece appearing in the publication, Sanjibani, he wrote: 'The Sanjibani pronounces in its last issue against Mr Tilak, on the ground that he is unpopular. But unpopular with whom? With a certain section of the old Congress's leaders... Mr Gokhale (Gopal Krishna Gokhale was a leading Congress politician who was known as a moderate. He has been often contrasted with Tilak; Stanley Wolpert's book, Tilak and Gokhale, is a study in that direction), for instance, is by no means popular in his own country, the Deccan, especially since his notorious apology... Yet none dreamed of opposing his selection to the presidential chair on the mere ground of a partial unpopularity.'[51] Thus, Sri Aurobindo left none in doubt about his leanings in favour of Tilak and his politics. His support extended to the likes of Bipin Chandra Pal, fellow contemporary of Tilak, whose views he gave prominence in Karmayogin.[52]

Between 1910 and 1950, until his death, Sri Aurobindo produced a stupendous array of intellectual material which transformed Indian consciousness and, very importantly, contextualized Hinduism in a way that was truly 'Indian'. While appreciative of Annie Besant's theosophical movement, he had his reservations on its success. 'I admit the truths that Theosophy seeks to unveil; but I do not think they can breached if we fall in bondage even to the most inspiring table talk of Mahatmas or to the confused anathemas and vaticinations hurled from their platform tripods by modern Pythonesses of the type of Mrs Annie Besant, that great, capacious but bewildered and darkened intellect, now stumbling with a loud

---

[51]ibid
[52]'Karmayogin', *The Complete Works of Sri Aurobindo*, Volume 8, 1997

and confident blindness through those worlds of twilight and glamour, of distorted inspirations, perverted communications and misunderstood or half-understood perceptions which are so painfully familiar to the student and seeker.'[53] Thus rejecting theosophy, he presented his solution: 'I seek a light that shall be new, yet old, the oldest indeed of all lights... I seek a text and a Shastra that is not subject to interpolation, modification and replacement... In short, I seek not science, not religion, not Theosophy, but Veda—the truth about Brahman, not only about His essentiality, but about His manifestation... I believe that Veda to be the foundation of the Santana Dharma; I believe it to be the concealed divinity within Hinduism...'[54] It is evident that his spiritual thoughts were never far from Hinduism, and that he placed in them complete trust to reveal the path of Truth. Consider this: 'The Vedanta, that solemn affirmation of the ultimate truths beyond which no human thinking has ever proceeded or can proceed, looking deep into the last recesses where existence take refuge from the scrutiny of the Mind, affirms there as the beginning and the end of all possible description of the infinite Knowable-Unknowable three terms, Being, Comprehension and Delight... From them all phenomena proceed, to them all phenomena seek to return.'[55]

The reach and reputation of Swami Vivekananda, Tilak and Sri Aurobindo and their religious-spiritual-political thoughts have continued well beyond their life-time. This was made possible largely because of individuals and organizations that idolised and eulogised them, and considered them moulders of

---

[53]'Essays Divine and Human', *The Complete Works of Sri Aurobindo*, Volume 12, 1997
[54]ibid
[55]ibid

the Hindu consciousness. One such individual was Hanuman Prasad Poddar, and one such organization was the Gita Press, which he co-founded.

FIVE

A Publisher Gets it Right

*The happiness which comes from long practice, which leads
to the end of suffering, which at first is like poison, but
at last like nectar—this kind of happiness arise from
the serenity of one's own mind.*

BHAGAVAD GITA

Barely three years after Tilak's death, a silent revolution came to be born, which was to dramatically transform the Hindu landscape. The Vedas, Upanishads, Puranas, Ramayana, Mahabharata and *Bhagavad Gita* had become popular literature, but they were either heavily priced or the quality of material in the market was below par. Here was a classic situation where the consumer was there but the right product was not. As a result of the missionary work done by Adi Shankaracharya, Ramanuja and Swami Vivekananda among others, a heightened awareness about Hindu identity had been created and there was renewed eagerness among the people to lay hands on the sacred texts. The aim was two-fold. One, to be better informed; after all, it would not do for a committed Hindu to demonstrate ignorance on the basics of his epics and scriptures. The second was to not be left out in the race to claim—proudly—the Hindu credentials. It is akin to laying hands on a Nobel Prize-winning author's work even if one understands little of literature, merely for the sake of dropping names in socialite circles. Two gentlemen, Jaydayal Goyandka and Hanuman Prasad Poddar, got together to meet this need. They established Gita Press, which took on the task of publishing Hindu books in various Indian languages at affordable prices. Given that they were Marwaris, one would be tempted to compliment their keen sense of business acumen, using a mix of scale and price-competitiveness. The fact, however, is that it was not business, but a religious calling, which made them plunge into the task of publishing. That they made good business out of it is incidental.

To understand the role the Gorakhpur-based Gita Press has played in promoting Hindu religious and political consciousness, here are some facts: As of early 2014, Gita Press had sold 72 million copies of the Gita; 70 million copies of poet-devotee Tulsidas's works; and 19 million copies of scriptures such as the Puranas and the Upanishads.[1] It also publishes two magazines— *Kalyan* in Hindi and *Kalyana-Kalpataru* in English—that have circulations of 200,000 and 100,000-plus respectively.[2] The phenomenal reach was well used by Gita Press to press ahead with its agenda of protecting and promoting Hindu values, goading fence-sitters to take sides, and providing a platform for various Hindu nationalist leaders in politics and outside to reach out to the masses. Gita Press did not shy from taking strong positions on issues such as the Hindu Code Bill, cow slaughter, and Hindu-Muslim relations both in the social and the political sense. It was also nimble-footed in identifying credible voices in Hindi literature and persuading them to write for its publications, as the reach of the Hindi language was phenomenal even if one takes into account the low percentage

---

[1] *Gita Press and the Making of Hindu India*; Akshaya Mukul; HarperCollins Publishers India, 2015
[2] ibid

of literacy in the 1920s-30s. (Even at the end of the British rule it was a mere 12 per cent.) While it is true that a number of its contributors came from the strident Hindu nationalist section, there were the 'moderates' who wrote; Mahatma Gandhi contributed too. 'It (Gita Press) was a crucial cog in the wheel of Hindu nationalism that struck up alliances with everyone: mendicants, liberals, politicians, philanthropists, scholars, sectarian organizations like the RSS, Hindu Mahasabha, Jana Sangh and VHP, and many conservative elements within the Congress.'[3] Now nearing 100 years of its existence, Gita Press has become the world's largest publisher of religious texts,[4] and the only other publishing organization that can be compared to this monolith is the US-based Zondervan Publishing House, which publishes the Bible in over 60 countries and in about 200 languages. Critics over the years have condemned Gita Press as an organization that has fanned communal divides in the name of promoting Hinduism and given space to extremist elements, but they cannot run away from the reality that the publishing house has contributed to the sharpening of the Hindu identity and making such identity coterminous with national interests.

There is very little material available in the public domain about Gita Press, though its success is there for all to see. One reason for the drought is that the founders of Gita Press, particularly Hanuman Prasad Poddar, staunchly believed in work without publicity. It is in this backdrop that Akshaya Mukul's book[5] becomes a valuable source of credible information, though one can quibble over the author's slant. The story of Gita Press is also the story of Hanuman Prasad Poddar, who became a

[3]ibid
[4]*Encyclopaedia Britannica*
[5]*Gita Press and the Making of Hindu India*, Akshaya Mukul, 2015

legend, both among his admirers and opponents. He was not just the organization's public face but also edited the influential Kalyan. Poddar was a nationalist, fired by a zeal to see India regain its ancient glory as a Hindu nation. Whether utopian or dangerous, his dream triggered commitment, and led him to doggedly pursue through the Gita Press and its magazines the goal of a Hindu India. That ultimate aim was not to be realized, but he certainly ended up establishing on a mass scale a mindset that made it possible for various Hindu nationalist leaders in the political sphere at that time, to win public support. As a Marwari businessman and a spiritualist, Poddar deftly used the prevailing socio-political situation to gain readership for his magazines and the various publications of Gita Press. Those were years of frequent communal disturbances involving the Hindu and the Muslim communities. Cow slaughter and loud music played from mosques—incidentally, issues that are exploited even today—became flashpoint matters. Poddar took an active part in various movements that promoted a ban on cow slaughter.

More importantly, he came to be increasingly seen in the camp of Congress leaders who were disturbed over the 'moderate' response from their party's top brass to minority provocation. That Poddar would also gravitate towards prominent figures in the All India Hindu Mahasabha, the Rashtriya Swayamsevak Sangh and the Bharatiya Jana Sangh—which was to later become the Bharatiya Janata Party—did not come as a surprise. The mix ensured that Poddar would have a foothold in all those organizations which strongly espoused the Hindu cause. 'Hindu nationalists used Kalyan's reach among Hindu reading public to the full, with Gita Press and Poddar as willing partners. Disillusioned with what he called the anti-Hindu policies of the first Congress government, the clear option for Poddar was to openly support, and even get actively involved in, the politics and struggles of Hindu nationalist groups and later political parties like the Jana Sangh.'[6]. His achievement was significant, considering that even at that point, his publications were using articles written by the likes of Mahatma Gandhi and S Radhakrishnan, besides usual suspects such as the RSS's M.S. Golwalkar.[7]

Even as he remained gleefully occupied with his pet themes of opposing cow slaughter, promoting Hindu epics and scriptures etc, Poddar found time to turn his attention on another 'threat': That of communism. The Communists in the twenties and the thirties of the 20th century were technically rivals of the Congress, but they were also alike. They were opposed to the Hindu groups and were seen as appeasers of the Muslim community. Besides, senior leaders of the Congress, Jawaharlal Nehru included, were viewed as being Left-oriented. Also, the Communists had scant regard for religion—and this was revolting to a deeply religious Poddar. Thus, for the Gita Press founder, there was little to differentiate between the Congress and the Left, especially when it came to Hindu-related issues. Finally, there was also a non-religious ideology at play. The Communists opposed capitalism and private enterprise. The Marxists among them, especially, were convinced that the capitalist system was the root cause of the world's misery and that a system run by the proletariat was the ideal solution. The Communists had failed where they were supposed to have succeeded the most, going by their theory:

[6] ibid
[7] *The Hindu Nationalist Movement in India*; Christophe Jaffrelot; Columbia University Press, 1998

The West, where, according to them, worker exploration as a result of the industrial revolution had been the most. But while western nations rejected them, communism found roots in countries such as China and Russia, which had missed the industrialization bus at that point in time and were largely agro-based. Communists, therefore, were eager to make up for the loss, and believed India provided that opportunity. Gita Press was a private enterprize, and a religious one at that. There wasn't a chance that either the Communists would back it or that Poddar and his team would endorse the Left. The sum was that the Leftists got added to Gita Press and company's List of the Unwanted.

BIZARRE YET EFFECTIVE

And yet, Gita Press was not averse to some fantastic stretches of imagination and frolic in order to pay the Communists back in their coin, so long as those efforts furthered the promotion of Hindu deities. In its publications, it indulged in 'bizarre' comparisons 'when it came to listing the forces behind the ancient godly Indian communism and the modern godless Russian communism. On the Indian side, it was a crowded list including Arjun, Yudhishthir, Vidhur, Vyas, Narada, Tulsidas, Chaitanya Maha Prabhu, Mirabai, Guru Nanak, Sant Tukaram, Ramdas...and others. How and why these mythological and real characters—epic heroes, poets, seers, and religious gurus—were chosen as the founding fathers of Indian communism is not known, but the list was certainly weightier compared to the three masterminds of Russian communism: Lenin, Trotsky and later Stalin.'[8] Mukul takes particular pleasure in expanding

---

[8]*Gita Press and the Making of Hindu India*, Akshaya Mukul, 2015

upon this ridiculous proposition—just who in the Gita Press group had got this brainwave is a mystery. 'Two similarities were noted between the Indian and Russian communism. The first would delight even the most serious of political theorists: it said that Lord Krishna, the originator of Indian communism, dallied with gopis—hardworking milkmaids—just as the fathers of Russian communism were involved with humble peasants and workers. The second similarity was more to the point: that both versions were aimed at the betterment of the poor and the downtrodden.'[9]

Jokes apart, Gita Press was immersed in the very serious work of shaping the Hindu consciousness through the books it published and the magazines it circulated. They were masterpieces in journalism to the extent that they were focused, and targeted at very specific readers. There was never any ambiguity, nor did Poddar and his team waver from their resolve and belief that their mandate was to satisfy the cravings of a large section of the Hindu community which had begun to feel short-changed. When praise came his way—from the likes of Mahatma Gandhi even[10]—he took it with humility, and when criticism was directed at him, he took it in his stride as the price one would pay in the noble task of keeping the Hindu pride alive. Born to a well-to-do Marwari family, Poddar could have, like many of his contemporary Marwaris, settled down in some business—tentative efforts had been made in the early years of his career to make him set base in what was

---

[9]ibid

[10]ibid. 'Personally Gandhi was extremely fond of Poddar. In a 1935 letter from Wardha, Gandhi expressed "happiness and satisfaction" with Poddar's views. "Sometimes I feel a man like you should stay with me… What you are doing through *Kalyan* and Gita Press is a great service to god. I feel I am part of what you are doing."'

then Bombay, by industrialist Jamnalal Bajaj.[11] Even so, he was regularly engaged in religious discourses organized here and there. He was also dogged by a string of personal calamities, but 'personal tragedies, minor or major, would not deter Poddar from his public role, be it as a prominent figure in the Marwari world—their business, social or even private space—or at the national level on diverse issues...'[12] If Mahatma Gandhi was one admirer of *Kalyan*, Golwalkar was another, and the two could not have been more different, although both these leaders shared an innate faith in the Hindu religion and its teachings. The RSS chief dwelt on 'true nationalism' in one of the articles he contributed to *Kalyan*. Speaking highly of a special issue of the magazine that dealt with Hindu culture, Golwalkar wrote to the editor, 'The off-tracked Hindu...of today should study this (*Hindu Sanskriti Ank*) and realize the greatness of his life. Once the realization sets in, he would discard (his) un-Indian belief system.'[13]

But while the objective of Gita Press remained unambiguously the promotion of Hindu faith and way of living, the publishing house was not averse to seeking out contributors from different religions and ideologies. These writers came from diverse backgrounds and could be social workers, spiritual gurus, scholars, politicians, and journalists so long as they had something complimentary to say about Hinduism. A few foreign contributors too were roped in to give an 'international' touch—one such person being Alexander Phipps, who studied in England, came to India during the Second World War, had a chance meeting with Ramana Maharishi, and was rechristened

---

[11]ibid
[12]ibid
[13]ibid

Madhava Ashish.[14] Sri Aurobindo and the Mother together contributed more than fifty articles to Kalyan;[15] ISKCON founder Swami Prabhupada was another contributor. Mahatma Gandhi, C Rajagopalachari and Annie Besant too wrote for *Kalyan*. Gita Press occupied an important place in the hearts of both the Mahatma and Madan Mohan Malaviya, though the latter did not write much for it. 'Poddar would later admit, "He (Malaviya) never used to give a categorical answer to requests for contribution. He was very good at talking, not so much at writing."'[16] Akshaya Mukul records in his book an interesting anecdote of Poddar's distaste for the high-profile Mahesh Yogi. Poddar believed that Mahesh Yogi's methods were 'a deviation from the well-laid-out shastric path and a threat to Sanatan Hindu dharma.'[17] One contributor with whom Poddar stuck a deep relationship, according to the author, was Rajendra Prasad. There was a 'high level of mutual admiration'. As President, Rajendra Prasad had inaugurated Gita Press's new building in 1955. It is evident from this eclectic sample that Poddar and Gita Press had no qualms in entertaining contributors whose socio-political positions may have conflicted with one another—there couldn't be two persons more different than Golwalkar and Gandhi, for instance, or Syama Prasad Mookerjee and Vinoba Bhave, both of whom wrote for *Kalyan*. The one person who kept his distance from Gita Press was Jawaharlal Nehru. 'Let alone an article, Nehru refused to send even a short message when requested by Poddar for the *Hindu Sanskriti Ank*, and again for the *Manavta Ank*.'[18] Was he driven by principles or arrogance?

---

[14]ibid
[15]ibid
[16]ibid
[17]ibid
[18]ibid

The world of literature has always played an important role in shaping and arousing public opinion on a variety of issues, be it the freedom movement or religion or political ideology. In India, the Left establishment has had a head start here. Since before Independence, and more so in the decades thereafter of the Nehruvian age, Left-Leaning figures have seeped into multiple organizations, ranging from literature to art to academics to even trade unions. It is only now, over the last few years, that the Leftist hegemony is being seriously challenged and alternative narratives are getting prominence. Given the Hindu-Hindi juxtaposition in north India, Poddar was understandably anxious that the Hindi literary world acknowledge Gita Press's contribution, both in terms of its religious might as well as the quality of literature. But Poddar was not very successful. 'Gita Press's mission of defending and disseminating Sanatan Hindu dharma and addressing the question of cultural and political identity failed to cut much ice with the leaders of the Hindi movement.'[19] The cause of this setback can be partly attributed to the hold of Communists in Hindi literature.[20] Interestingly though, although Poddar and Premchand had little in common by way of ideology, the celebrated Hindi litterateur wrote for *Kalyan*. 'He (Premchand) and Poddar were comfortable with each other.'[21]

---

[19]ibid

[20]Surendra Chowdhury's article, 'Decades of Ideological Cold War and Hindi Literature', gives valuable insight on the subject. Events such as the October Revolution, the Naxalite phenomenon, the growing class struggles across India, and the fascination of the 'intellectuals' towards Marxism had greatly influenced thought processes soon after independence. Titans in Hindi literature, such as Premchand, H.S. Vatsyayana, Yashpal, Dharamvir Bharati etc, moved by the social order of the day, would have given little attention to the Gita Press's efforts.

[21]*Gita Press and the Making of Hindu India*, Akshaya Mukul, 2015

In most tellings of the Hindu story in India over the centuries, perhaps Gita Press would occupy not even a footnote, assuming somebody remembers. The irony is that most academics that render such narrations would have known or come across editions of the vastly circulated Hindu sacred books or magazines published by this organization. But they remain unaware of the monumental impact Gita Press has had on the Hindu mind. Arguably, but for Hanuman Prasad Poddar and his organization, a number of national leaders, especially belonging to the Right, would not have captured the public imagination like they did from the 1930s on—which was also when Gita Press and *Kalyan* began soaring in the sky.

SIX

Two Men and Their Organization Arrive

All the time, circumstances are not going to favour us. We shall have to face obstacles and adversities. Fearlessness is the first virtue of a hero, the starting point of all other noble virtues.

— M.S. GOLWALKAR

E ven as Hanuman Prasad Poddar and his Gita Press publications were reaching millions of Hindu homes and re-energizing their religious identity—something that, decades later, the televized serials on Mahabharata and Ramayana would achieve in their own unique ways—a new crop of organizations and their leaders had emerged on the national scene that would significantly enhance the 'Hindu nation' idea. They had aggression and unflagging commitment, which helped them draw hordes of supporters and sympathizers in the years to come. Further, these leaders and their outfits changed the very discourse of not just the Hindu-ness of India, but also the political response to it. During the freedom struggle, they linked the campaign to the anti-British rule movement, claiming that a Hindu nation could not remain subservient to foreign rule—more so a rule which professed a faith that was an import and not Indic in nature. These organizations and their key driving forces had also another target—the Muslim population, which was seen as not fully aligned to the idea of a Hindu oneness and which refused to accept the notion that they had a common cultural lineage with their majority Hindu brethren. Of course, none of these outfits accepted that they were anti-Muslim in the same way that they were anti-British reign, but they made it clear that the Hindu identity superseded all other claims, and those few ones from other faiths who happened to back the idea were quickly co-opted as 'true nationalists'. The foremost among these organizations was the Rashtriya Swayamsevak Sangh. It was around the time that Gita Press was finding its métier that the RSS came into being. There were several reasons which facilitated its arrival and subsequent astounding growth.

Lokmanya Tilak had died in 1920, and Sri Aurobindo had withdrawn from revolutionary politics. But the spirit of their zeal and pride in being a Hindu lived on. Meanwhile, the Hindu-Muslim confrontation had taken a serious turn with the Shuddhi versus Tabligh clash.[1] The Arya Samaj, led by Swami Shradhanand, heralded a movement to reconvert those who had left the Hindu fold to join Islam but still clung on to various Hindu customs. On the other hand, the Muslim religious leaders—the various Ulemas—launched the tabligh drive, aimed at ensuring that such Muslim converts were not lured back into the Hindu fold. Both sides used provocative measures and the result was a charged communal environment, leading to frequent violence. The agenda of reconversion and blocking the move needed more than individual effort; an organized method had to be employed for long-term success. Prominent leaders such as Madan Mohan Malviya, B.S. Moonje and Lala Lajpat Rai strongly advocated the formation of a 'sangathan' to take the

---

[1]*RSS's Tryst with Politics: From Hedgewar to Sudarshan*; Pralay Kanungo; Manohar Publishers and Distributors, Reprinted in 2017

cause forward.[2] The sangathan would not just keep an eye on converts, to get them purified at the first available opportunity and brought back into the Hindu fold, but also work towards promoting Hindu consciousness in a more strident way. Leader after leader reminded his audience that the Hindus had been at the receiving end of Muslim violence because they were unprepared to use force if necessary (while the Muslims were always better equipped, both materially and temperamentally). The 1921 Malabar uprising was cited as one such instance. It began as a peasant rebellion against the British by the Mappila in the southern region of Malabar, triggered by the British crackdown on the Khilafat movement, but soon turned into mass atrocity against the Hindus by the Muslim Mappilas. A shocked Annie Besant wrote: 'They murdered and plundered abundantly, and killed and drove away all Hindus who would not apostate. Somewhere about a lakh of people were driven from their homes with nothing but the clothes they had on, stripped of everything. Malabar has taught us what Islamic rule still means, and we do not want to see another specimen of the Khilafat Raj in India.'[3]

The sangathan, therefore, decided to impart physical training to its people. Interestingly, this drive attracted people from various parties, such as the Congress and the Hindu Mahasabha. It must be remembered here that the Khilafat movement had been supported by Mahatma Gandhi, much to the concern of many Congressmen, and his stand must have contributed to the later opposition by Hindu outfits and so-called extremists to his 'appeasement' methods. While the Hindu organizations,

---

[2]ibid
[3]*The Future of Indian Politics: A Contribution to the Understanding of Present-Day Problems*; Annie Besant; Theosophical Publishing House, 1922

determined to ensure a non-repeat of the Malabar type incident, went about reframing their response, the Muslim outfits weren't sitting idle. The tanzim was initiated in 1923 by its leaders, most prominent among them being S. Kitchlew.[4] He appealed to various Muslim organizations, charitable bodies, banks, etc., to join hands and fund the tanzim. He even launched an Urdu daily with the same name, which published anti-Hindu articles. But for once, the reach and scale of the Muslim initiative could not match that of the Hindus' sangathan.[5] The success of the sangathan coupled with a burning desire to 'show the Muslims their place' and aggressively promote nationalism as inherent to Hinduism, propelled the formation of the RSS on that Dussehra day in 1925, though it was named thus a few months later on Ram Navami in 1926. The formation of shakhas (or branches), the inculcation of deep reverence for Mother India, the physical training (represented by baton-wielding RSS workers at the training camps), and the repeated reminders of being Hindu (by religion, by nationhood, by cultural history), were to become the RSS's hallmark. They also drew criticism: RSS's opponents said the organization promoted violence and communal divide. But the die was cast—five people led by Keshav Baliram Hedgewar got together in Nagpur to establish the RSS, with Hedgewar becoming its first head. Among the founders was Babarao Savarkar, brother of Vinayak Damodar 'Veer' Savarkar. The choice of the outfit's name was interesting: It brought in nationalism and voluntariness but did not deem it necessary to overstate its pro-Hindu credentials in its name. Perhaps this was because the use of the 'Hindu' word could have made it sound like the other important organization, Hindu

---

[4]*RSS's Tryst with Politics: From Hedgewar to Sudarshan*, Pralay Kanungo, 2002
[5]ibid

Mahasabha, which already existed. Or perhaps it had plotted a more inclusive agenda for itself, to the extent of equating Hindu-ness with India. The new chief insisted on having the slogan, *Bharat Mata Ki Jai*, alongside the prayers at the end of every shakha meeting—and this was his way of merging Hindu with nationhood.[6] Whatever the case may have been, the omission was not to in any way diminish the RSS's pro-Hindu reputation—its vision of the Hindu ideology driving a united and free India.

HEDGEWAR: DOCTOR-TURNED HINDU ACTIVIST

Hedgewar's nationalistic fervour had been evident in his school days when he was rusticated for leading a Vande Mataram movement.[7] Later in life, he drew inspiration from Tilak and B.S. Moonje, who became his guru of sorts. Moonje had built a reputation for himself as a hardliner when it came to the projection of Hindu rights and zero-compromise with the British. Moonje had been a strong Tilak supporter and had sided with him during critical moments, including at the Congress party's annual conference in Surat in 1907. He founded the Bhonsale Military School in Nashik to impart military training to Hindu youth. Hedgewar's task was cut out and he went about with single-minded focus. There was no time to be lost—the Hindus had to be mobilized effectively, the Muslims were to be made to understand that they could not take the majority religion for granted, and the British were to be pressured into leaving. If the RSS faltered in any of these steps, it would be

[6]*Khaki Shorts and Saffron Flags: A Critique of the Hindu Right*; Tapan Basu, Pradip Datta, Sumit Sarkar, Tanika Sarkar, Sambuddha Sen; Orient Blackswan, 1993
[7]*RSS's Tryst with Politics: From Hedgewar to Sudarshan,* Pralay Kanungo, 2002

not just the end of the organization but also a betrayal of the very core ideals of millions of Hindus. Hedgewar had studied medicine and graduated as a doctor, and so he would often apply logic to his thought processes. According to RSS literature— there are far too many, churned out in enormous quantities by various units of the organization spread across the country, to list them here—Hedgewar asked himself the question: How could the Hindus, who have had a glorious past stretching from ancient to medieval times, so abjectly surrender to Muslim rulers, whether Turks, Afghans or Mughals? How could they then allow themselves to be enslaved by the British? They had muscle power, they had money power, they had intellect; what they lacked, according to Hedgewar, was a sense of Hindu consciousness and cohesion.[8] Developing those qualities was to become the RSS's mandate. Hedgewar took another key decision: That of keeping the RSS away from active politics. He must have believed that politics would lead his organization to the sort of compromises that he wanted it to keep away from, at least in those initial decades. He was certainly more glued to the concept of Hindu Rashtra than Hindu Rajya, believing that the second would follow the realization of the first. Thus, certain decisions he took in that direction have been viewed by his and the RSS's critics today as evidence that while the RSS claims to be nationalistic, it had kept away from the independence movement. Here is one instance: 'Mahatma Gandhi gave a call for Satyagraha against the British government. Gandhi himself launched the Salt Satyagraha, undertaking his Dandi Yatra. Dr Hedgewar decided to participate only individually and not let the RSS join the freedom movement officially. He sent information everywhere that the Sangh will not participate in the Satyagraha.

---

[8]ibid

However, those wishing to participate individually in it were not prohibited.' He spent nine months in jail as a result of his role.[9]

Two years before the Quit India Movement was launched, Hedgewar breathed his last, and his final message to the swayamsevaks was: 'I see before my eyes today a miniature Hindu Rashtra.'[10] His confidence came from the exponential expansion of the RSS during his lifetime. In 1931, the organization had just 60 shakhas; by 1936 it had 200 branches and 25,000 members; by 1939, the numbers had risen to 500 and 40,000 respectively. In the year of Hedgewar's death, the RSS had 700 shakhas and 80,000 members.[11] Hedgewar had thus effectively prepared the ground for a robust organization that would be capable of taking on its critics and strengthening the discourse on Hinduism and Hindutva. But while Hedgewar's ideology and strategy were unambiguous, the argumentative edge and the precision needed to counter rivals on an intellectual plane was lacking. His successor, Madhav Sadashiv Golwalkar, rose to the occasion.

THE GOLWALKAR ERA

'Guru' Golwalkar (he taught at the Benaras Hindu University, and thus the prefix) was an unlikely candidate to succeed Hedgewar. He was not among the Sangh seniors, had an inclination towards spiritual inward-looking rather than community-building, and generally kept to himself—not a good sign for a potential leader of a cadre-based organization. But he

---

[9]*Religion, Power & Violence: Expression of Politics in Contemporary Times*; Edited by Ram Puniyani; SAGE India, 2005
[10]*RSS's Tryst with Politics: From Hedgewar to Sudarshan*, Pralay Kanungo, 2002
[11]ibid

had the advantage of being close to the founder-chief. Besides, 'One possible explanation is that Hedgewar was frustrated by the endless bickering among Hindu Mahasabha stalwarts... Therefore, he was keen to detach the RSS from the Hindu Mahasabha despite their ideological proximity and wanted a successor who would effectively keep his organization away from these Mahasabha leaders.'[12] Golwalkar met this criterion, as he was not close to the Mahasabha leaders. Golwalkar was erudite and a thinker. That he was a cut above the rest was soon to be evident in his writings and style of leadership. Some of his decisions drew the ire of nationalists of that time, and his rivals. One of these was to keep the RSS and its members away from the freedom movement. He also heeded the call of the British regime, caught in the vortex of the Second World War, for an end to military drills and wearing of military or military-kind uniforms by civilian outfits, and directed all RSS branches to discontinue the practice. His directives did create temporary discontent with in the organization, 'but Golwalkar was determined to adopt this strategy in order to avoid British ire and expand the organization quietly, avoiding any public controversy.'[13]

The new RSS chief's decisions must have certainly brought relief to the British, who were none too eager to take on the monolith that the RSS had become by then, and add to their already considerable troubles. These moves have been analysed in later years as evidence of the RSS not participating in the freedom struggle and thus helping the British. But Golwalkar was clear on his motive: He had to consolidate Hindu power, and this could not be done by confronting the government

---

[12]ibid
[13]ibid

every now and then. He had to work silently and wait for the right occasion to strike. 'Golwalkar's outward compliance with government orders was no more than a smoke-screen behind which to carry on secretly or in a modified form the very activities that he had renounced.'[14] The RSS chief was not against the Independence movement, but he saw no merit in antagonizing the foreign rulers to the detriment of Hindu interests. In this, he appeared to have followed Tilak's public position on reforms within Hindu society, when the Lokmanya publicly opposed such reforms despite being personally in favour of them, because he feared the reform drive would take attention away from the freedom struggle. Also, in seeking to discontinue—at least for some time—the militant drills, Golwalkar was giving expression of his individualistic belief that the most important task at hand was the intellectual and moral uplift of the Hindu community in order to equip them to take on their opponents. The British were of course shrewd enough to realise the plan. Author Pralay Kanungo notes from government records: 'Their (RSS) policy is to wait until they themselves are better prepared and the state of the country offers better opportunities for intervention...the Sangh, though not now dangerous, might become a menace later in times of serious communal disturbances, etc.'[15]

Two far-reaching events occurred during Golwakar's reign: Mahatma Gandhi's assassination and the country's partition. The first came as a major blow to the RSS's image, since the impression got created, which the RSS then did little to dispel, that the outfit was complicit in the murder—the killer Nathuram Godse had been with the RSS but went over to the

---

[14]ibid
[15]ibid

Hindu Mahasabha; he was not an RSS member at the time he committed the crime. The RSS was banned, for the first though not the last time. Salt was rubbed on the wound when the supposedly pro-Hindu Sardar Vallabhbhai Patel took a dim view of the activities of the Sangh; the ban came during the Sardar's term as the country's Home Minister. A little over a year later, the ban was lifted after the RSS committed itself to a written constitution and transparency. The partition took the RSS by surprise, because the organization had not anticipated the British move to quit the country in this manner.[16] The Hindu outfit squarely blamed Mahatma Gandhi and his 'dangerously naive' approach to the Muslims for the resultant mass killings soon after partition.

It is interesting that, sensing the public mood, Golwalkar did not challenge the ban; instead he ordered the RSS branches to suspend all its activities for the time being. But he also launched efforts to build bridges with the Nehru government. In a letter to Sardar Patel, he raised the 'menace' of communism getting the upper hand, and said, 'I for one feel that if you with government power and we with organised cultural force combine, we can soon eliminate this menace.'[17] Clearly, Golwalkar was playing on Sardar Patel's dislike of the Communists.

There was also a third crucial development during Golwalkar's tenure: The launch of the Bharatiya Jana Sangh. The RSS was not willing to take the political plunge, but many of its influential members were keen about politics. The formation of the BJS— which was to later become the BJP—came about as a result of these sentiments. The BJS became the political arm of the RSS, and its first head was Syama Prasad Mookerjee. Golwalkar

---

[16]*Rashtriya Swayamsevak Sangh*; D.R. Goyal; South Asia Books, 1979
[17]*RSS's Tryst with Politics: From Hedgewar to Sudarshan*, Pralay Kanungo, 2002

turned down Mookerjee's suggestion to bring the RSS into the new political outfit's ambit, but agreed to depute some of its 'staunch and tried' workers to guide the new party.[18] The RSS chief, however, realised that the goal of spreading Hindu-ness needed more organizations. Thus came the establishment of the Bharatiya Mazdoor Sangh—the Akhil Bhartiya Vidyarthi Parishad had already been formed to draw in the youth to the RSS fold. That Golwalkar was willing to forgo, even if for a short duration, confrontation with known enemies for the larger good of the RSS, was best seen when the RSS vociferously backed Indira Gandhi's call to sink differences and meet the Pakistani challenge in 1971. This not only presented the organization in good light before the prime minister, but also boosted the RSS's patriotic credentials among the people, which had taken a knock with Mahatma Gandhi's assassination and its failure to anticipate the country's partition and do anything to stop the related massacres.

FIREBRAND HINDUISM

Through all these manoeuvrings, Golwalkar remained focussed on the larger goal of promoting Hindu pride and Hindu Rashtra. Besides regularly fine-tuning the organization, he wrote profusely and with sharpness of intellect, which is evident in the *Bunch of Thoughts*—a collection of his writings on a variety of subjects. However, it was the publication of *We or Our Nationhood Defined* in 1939 that had catapulted him onto the national stage. It contained some explosive material, including tributes to Adolf Hitler and his drive for racial supremacy. It became a matter

---

[18]*The Jana Sangh: A Biography of an Indian Political Party*; Craig Baxter; Oxford University Press, 1967

of deep embarrassment for the RSS because the circulation of this work coincided with the start of the Second World War, and publicity about Hitler's dubious and dangerous theories and brutal reign. It was only two decades later that Golwalkar disclaimed authorship of the controversial work.[19] But the clarification failed to douse the fire, and to this date critics of the RSS refer to those writings and hold Golwalkar responsible for them, calling both him and the Sangh 'fascist and Hitlerian'. The RSS did not help matters by its overt belligerence in favour of Hindus, against the Muslims (the non-nationalist type, at any rate) and its leaning towards programmes and policies which seemed on the surface to create social and communal divides. In sum, though, if we have to gain an insight into Golwalkar's mind, it is best to refer to the *Bunch of Thoughts*[20] and not the material whose authorship remains contested. Four points in it readily spring to mind: One, that while Mahatma Gandhi had a proper cultural concept of India, he chose the wrong person (Jawaharlal Nehru) to represent it; two, the Father of the Nation's support to the Khilafat movement was a huge mistake; three, unlike the shakhas, the Huns and others, the Muslims in India failed to assimilate into the national mainstream because they never considered themselves to be part of the Indian nationhood; and four, the RSS was against all kinds of caste and class divisions in Hindu society. Two other important observations, important because they came to form a consistently projected narrative of the RSS in the decades that followed, were: Leaders of the freedom movement continued to give concessions to the Muslim minority at the cost of the

---

[19]*RSS's Tryst with Politics: From Hedgewar to Sudarshan*, Pralay Kanungo, 2002
[20]*Bunch of Thoughts*; M.S. Golwalkar; Vikrama Prakashan; Fourth Impression, December 1968

majority Hindus in the vain hope that they could win over the former; and, Hindu nationalism was not the kind of chauvinistic call generally associated with Hitler or Benito Mussolini, but one that taught loyalty and devotion to Mother India.

Golwalkar tackled materialism from the Hindu prism, saying that the Hindu faith offered a solution to achieving the 'inner bond of unity'. He said, 'Our ancient Hindu philosophers, therefore, had turned their gaze to a plane higher than materialism. They delved deep into mysteries of the human soul...and discovered the Ultimate Reality.'[21] He then lamented that 'such a glorious heritage is being condemned and brushed aside by its own children. It has become a fashion these days to deride our ancient ideals and traditions and talk of recasting our society in the mould of other modern "isms".'[22] Further, he offered a solution: 'The Rashtriya Swayamsevak Sangh has resolved to fulfil that age-old mission by forging, as the first step, the present-day scattered elements of Hindu society into an organized and invincible force both on the place of the Spirit and on the plane of material life.'[23] Golwalkar hailed Hindu philosophy, which he said had 'pictured the highest state of society and given its cogent explanation too.'[24]

Golwalkar does not, in the above instance, speak of galvanizing Indian society, but Hindu society, because he found it in disarray and therefore unable to meet any challenges. In a bid to dispel the argument that talk of Hindu nation is driven by political considerations—which the RSS could not openly own

---

[21]'Our World Mission', *Bunch of Thoughts*, M.S. Golwalkar, Fourth Impression (1968)
[22]ibid
[23]ibid
[24]'Challenges of the Times', *Bunch of Thoughts*, M.S. Golwalkar, Fourth Impression (1968)

up to, since it professed to keep a distance from politics—he stated, 'Our concept of Hindu Nation is not a mere bundle of political and economic rights. It is essentially a cultural one... And it is only an intense rejuvenation of the spirit of our culture that can give us a true vision of our national life, and fruitful direction to all our efforts in solving the innumerable problems confronting our nation today.'[25] The RSS chief then decided to explain Hindu Culture. 'We feel it (Hindu Culture), though we cannot define it... Our culture, too, though, defying definition, has left its indelible stamp on all walks of life.'[26] Here, Golwalkar interestingly referred to Nehru, saying that he was in two minds on what should be done with the ashes of his wife who had died abroad. His intellect and modern education rebelled against immersing the ashes in the Triveni Sangam in Allahabad, but 'the ancient samskar won' and the ashes were indeed immersed in the waters at the holy confluence. 'This the imprint of culture,'[27] Golwalkar triumphantly remarked.

Over and over again in the collected writings, Golwalkar returned to his pet theme of the Hindu nation. 'Our one supreme goal is to bring to life the all-round glory and greatness of our Hindu Rashtra.'[28] The use of physical strength was necessary, he said, but 'character is more important. Strength without character will only make a brute of a man. Purity of character from the individual as well as the national standpoint is the real life-breath of national glory and greatness.'[29] Not

---

[25]'Call of Our National Soul', *Bunch of Thoughts*, M.S. Golwalkar, Fourth Impression (1968)
[26]ibid
[27]ibid
[28]'For True National Glory', *Bunch of Thoughts*, M.S. Golwalkar, Fourth Impression (1968)
[29]ibid

surprisingly, he fell back on a Hindu narration involving Prahlad and Indra. Expanding further on the subject of national glory, he said bluntly that a spirit of heroism is needed to achieve goals—'The spirit of heroism is necessary even to worship god. A coward cannot do it.'[30]

Having listed out the many merits of Hindu-ness and its inherent connect with nationhood, Golwalkar found it necessary to understand what 'Hindu' means. 'All the sects, the various castes in the Hindu fold, can be defined, but the term "Hindu" cannot be defined because it comprises all.'[31] He wondered: 'Is it that we are Hindus only by the force of circumstances or by "accident of birth"? Are we Hindu because have remained untouched by conversion to Islam or Christianity, as the proselytisers were few and we were very large in numbers? Is that the only meaning of our being Hindus? There is no use merely in saying, "Oh! We have a great culture." What do we know of it? How do we practise it? Let us gradually assimilate all those distinctive Hindu traits so that we can stand before the world as positive, dynamic Hindus. Let us live up to our philosophy, our dharma, and all those great qualities which have moulded our lives for countless generations.'[32]

Golwalkar sought to present the country as the mother of all Indians and exhorted everyone to worship it as one worships one's mother. This was clearly a matter of irritation to the Muslims who did not believe in idol (or form) worship. The Sangh chief made them squirm further when he stated that all religious events of the Hindus began with the bhoomi pujan

---

[30]ibid
[31]'Live Positive Dynamic Hinduism', *Bunch of Thoughts*, M.S. Golwalkar, Fourth Impression (1968)
[32]ibid

(worship of the Earth), which should remind every Hindu of the necessity to worship our nation too.[33] He then deftly brought in partition, and dismissed the talk that people on either side of the border remained brothers even after this division of land. 'Have we ever heard of children cutting up their mother, saying that she is their common property? What depths of depravity!'[34]

Here is another—and the last for our immediate purpose—passage from *Bunch of Thoughts* to round up Golwalkar's teachings and socio-political philosophy. On the sensitive Muslim question, he did not pull punches, quite aware that he was exposing himself to terrible condemnations of various kinds, from being parochial to communal to divisive to even dangerous for a country such as India with such dazzling diversity. He said: 'Then came the question of Muslims. They had come here as invaders. They were conceiving themselves as conquerors and rulers here for the last twelve hundred years. That complex was still in their mind. History has recorded that their antagonism was not merely political. Had it been so, they could have been won over in a very short time. But it was so deep-rooted that whatever we believe in, the Muslim was wholly hostile to it. If we worship in the temple, he would desecrate it... If we worship the cow, he would like to eat it. If we glorify a woman as a symbol of sacred motherhood, he would like to molest her...'[35] This was a load-full of exaggeration, and yet it was enthusiastically accepted by hundreds and thousands of Hindus in the country, because the level of appeasement that so-called secular parties had indulged in to keep the minorities humoured,

[33]'Our Motherland', *Bunch of Thoughts*, M.S. Golwalkar, Fourth Impression (1968)
[34]ibid
[35]'Territorial Nationalism', *Bunch of Thoughts*, M.S. Golwalkar, Fourth Impression (1968)

had angered them all. Golwalkar must have realised that he was over-stating matters, but he was also mindful that the points of Hindu-Muslim conflict which he had highlighted were not imaginary. He was able to strike a chord when he dramatically pilloried national 'secular' leaders: 'The Hindu was asked to ignore, even submit meekly to the vandalism and atrocities of the Muslims… If they carry away your wives and daughters, let them. Do not obstruct them. That would be violence!'[36] The biting sarcasm did not fail to find its target, and added to the Sangh's membership and branches.

Golwalkar passed away in 1973, at a time when Indira Gandhi was at her peak. Three years after his death, the government introduced the term 'secular' in the Preamble to the Constitution. It goes without saying that had he been around, we would have had yet another scathing commentary by him on the development. As things stood, an Internal Emergency had been imposed by Indira Gandhi by then, which had resulted in large-scale crackdowns on opposition political leaders and dissidents—real and suspected. Fundamental Rights had been suspended and Press censorship was put in place. How did the post-Golwalkar RSS respond to the developments? That was more to do with politics than Hinduism. Suffice it to say that the RSS's role remains a matter of conflicting opinions. Indira Gandhi's key aide, R.K. Dhawan, said that the RSS had not backed the Emergency. 'There was no such mention of the RSS supporting Indira Gandhi.'[37] On the other hand, former Intelligence Bureau chief T.V. Rajeswar had claimed the opposite. 'Not only were they (RSS) supportive of this, they wanted to establish contact apart from Mrs Gandhi, with

[36]ibid
[37]www.firstpost.com, September 24, 2015

Sanjay Gandhi also.'[38] Whatever the truth may have been, the RSS stuck to the path so clearly laid by Golwalkar.

Since the time it began its operations, the RSS has faced consistent criticism from a variety of quarters on account of its 'communal' nature. The hatred for the Sangh has bred an industry of academics and writers, some of whom have made careers out of pulping the organization and its star ideologue Golwalkar. Not all of the condemnations were unfair, even though they may have been driven by bias. The RSS did polarize society into 'us' versus 'they'—the 'us' being the Hindus and 'they' being primarily the Muslims. Moreover, the Sangh's call for a Hindu Rashtra unsettled even many Hindus who objected to their religion being dragged into the public sphere and who refused to buy into the nuances that RSS ideologues presented to justify their objective. Cultural nationalism was also a problem area for many who felt that diversity in religion and culture had served India well for centuries, and that a unitary cultural construct went against the grain of the 'unity in diversity' slogan. On the flip side, though, the others too had done no better. Under the garb of secularism—though the word had not yet made it to the Constitution of India—they had blatantly pursued appeasement of the minorities and considered every pro-Hindu remark as an assault on multiculturalism. Foremost, among these critics were those from the Left. It is no wonder that the RSS considered the Communists as much their rivals as the Muslim community. 'When he (Golwalkar) was imprisoned after Gandhi's assassination, he offered to Nehru and Patel that the government and the RSS should jointly fight the growing menace of communism. The Sino-Indian war of 1962 provided the immediate context to Golwalkar to club Communists with

---

[38]www.firstpost.com, September 22, 2015

Muslims and Christians.'[39] For good measure, he also tagged Communists with socialists and said they were all the same, at least in their political attitudes, and claimed that 'socialism and democracy are mutually contradictory' and that among the first victims of socialism is individual freedom.[40]

The Sangh chief had no love for Christians either, viewing them with deep suspicion. He said, 'So far as the Christians are concerned, to a superficial observer, they appear not only quite harmless but as the very embodiment of sympathy and love for humanity! Their speeches abound in words like "service" and "human salvation", as though they are specially deputed by the Almighty to uplift humanity! The people of our country, simple and innocent as they are, are taken in by all these...'[41] Here, Golwalkar helpfully gave an instance where a Christian missionary, in response to Rajendra Prasad's advice to avoid proselytisation and concentrate on social service, said that they were in the field primarily to increase the number of followers of Jesus Christ.[42] The RSS leader related his own interaction with a missionary who told him: 'Our aim is to knock out the faith from the heart of the Hindu. When his faith is shattered, his nationalism is also destroyed... Then it becomes easy for us to fill that void with Christianity.'[43] Golwalkar rebuked the practice and said that Christian missionaries had indulged in not just 'irreligious' but also 'anti-national' activities. At that point in time, he would have had many takers for his suspicion; the Niyogi committee report had been published by the Madhya

[39]*RSS's Tryst with Politics: From Hedgewar to Sudarshan*, Pralay Kanungo, 2002
[40]*Bunch of Thoughts*, M.S. Golwalkar, Fourth Impression (1968)
[41]'Internal Threats', *Bunch of Thoughts*, M.S. Golwalkar, Fourth Impression (1968)
[42]ibid
[43]ibid

Pradesh government in 1956, and its findings had clearly established the large-scale activities of Christian missionaries converting Hindus to their faith by dangling various carrots.[44]

Golwalkar may have been the first in his organization to precisely concretize the Hindu Rashtra idea along with the Hindu Identity, but he was not the first on the national stage to do so. The credit for that goes to Vinayak Damodar Savarkar.

---

[44]*Vindicated by Time: The Niyogi Committee Report on Christian Missionary Activities*; Voice of India, 1998. In his introduction to this edition, author and thinker Sita Ram Goel wrote the following: 'The Christian missionary orchestra in India after independence Independence has continued to rise from one crescendo to another with the applause of the Nehruvian establishment manned by a brood of self-alienated Hindus spawned by missionary-Macaulayite education.' The report had been deeply embarrassing for the Nehruvian regime, and the consequence was that the missionary activities got curbed to a great extent, although they did not stop altogether.

SEVEN

Hindutva Makes Its Debut by Name

It is not want of resources, O Hindus, which forces you to be so helpless and hopeless. But it is the want of practical insight in political realities to know your resources.

V.D. SAVARKAR

Hedgewar, and later Golwalkar, created a common perceptional construct that sought to equate and assimilate a range of Hindu concepts. Hindu, Hindu Identity, Hindu Nation, Nationalism, Patriotism—all of these were seen as not different from one another but synonymous to each other. However, such identification and seamless interlinkage had been proposed very strongly before these two RSS stalwarts by Vinayak Damodar Savarkar. It is possible that both Hedgewar and Golwalkar drew their inspiration from the position Savarkar had taken. Savarkar was the first Hindu ideologue to articulate this in detail, and with compelling arguments so strong that they continue to form the backbone of the Hindu cultural and political narrative to this date. He was a Tilakite in many ways, except that his literature on Hindu ideology brought forth the concept of Hindutva, arguably for the first time in the public domain.[1] Besides, being an important

---

[1]In his book, *RSS's Tryst with Politics* (2002), author Pralay Kanungo mentions Hindutva in the context of Golwalkar, but provides no citation for the information.

functionary of the Akhil Bharatiya Hindu Mahasabha, which had taken to politics unlike the RSS—though like the RSS it positioned itself as a protector of the Hindu community in the country—Savarkar was as deeply involved in the political as he was in the cultural arena from the 1920s. Such has been his stature that the Hindu Mahasabha is remembered by his name, and not the other way round. It is not a coincidence that the Mahasabha's influence fizzled out after Savarkar's death in 1966. Today, it exists only in name, and is a fringe player.

Two events determined the creation of the Hindu Mahasabha. The first was the formation of the All India Muslim League, which was to later successfully spearhead the demand for a Muslim nation carved out of India.[2] The second was the announcement of a separate electorate for Muslims as part of the Morley-Minto Reforms.[3] Prominent leaders, with Madan Mohan Malaviya being among them, were alarmed at the turn of events and interpreted the two developments as a danger sign for the Hindu community. As it is, they had been feeling disturbed by Muslim belligerence in various walks of life and what they saw as the British's leanings towards the minorities. A bunch of leaders, thus led by Malaviya and Lala Lajpat Rai,

---

[2]The All India Muslim League was formed in 1906 with the original aim of advocating the rights of the Muslim population. Its primary focus was to humour the landed gentry and the aristocratic sections of the minority community. The 'All India' tag was later shed after the league declared its resolve to fight for the creation of Pakistan under M.A. Jinnah.

[3]The Indian Councils Act of 1909, commonly referred to as the Morley-Minto Reforms, was a law passed by the British Parliament with a view to increasing the involvement of Indians in the governance of British India. The controversial provision in the Act was the grant of separate electorates for Muslims. Most historians believe that the decision was taken, in collaboration with certain Muslim leaders, to create a Hindu-Muslim divide and make it easier for the British to rule.

formed the Punjab Hindu Sabha in 1909, the year of the Morley-Minto Reforms. Despite its sectarian name (Punjab), the Sabha's leaders emphasized that it encompassed the entire Hindu community. A few conferences were organized of the new body in Punjab before its leaders took the decision to revamp the Sabha's structure and name. After five years of its existence, the Punjab Hindu Sabha was renamed as the Akhil Bharatiya Hindu Sabha, and it began to quickly expand beyond Punjab, but as various versions of the original. Eventually, it was decided sometime in 1915 to create a unified organization which would take into its fold the many Hindu Sabhas, and the final version came into being formally in 1916—though it was only in 1921 that the grouping of Hindu-centric people adopted the 'Mahasabha' name. There was no dispute over its principal role of promoting the interests of the Hindu population, but there were some differences over the position the new outfit should take with regard to the British rule—not to mention the Congress, given that many prominent leaders of the Mahasabha were leading Congress lights. Interestingly, Mahatma Gandhi was present at the event when the decision to launch an all-India Hindu Mahasabha was taken. From all accounts, he had been supportive of the Mahasabha's mandate to empower the Hindu community. Ironically, barely three decades later, one of the organization's extremist members assassinated Mahatma Gandhi, and the Mahasabha since 1948 has adopted a hateful position against the Father of the Nation—unveiling a statue of the killer, Nathuram Godse,[4] and laying the foundation stone for a temple to deify Godse.[5]

But the Hindu Mahasabha of 1916, and in the immediate

---

[4]www.firstpost.com, October 2, 2016
[5]www.huffingtonpost.com, November 16, 2017

successive years, certainly did not demonstrate any such venom. Ever since the 1920s, when it came under Savarkar's influence, the Akhil Bharatiya Hindu Mahasabha concentrated on consolidating Hindu support for its activities, lampooning the Congress and asking all and sundry to beware of the Muslims' anti-Hindu designs. While the outfit was deeply critical of Mahatma Gandhi's 'Muslim appeasement-based leadership'— with Savarkar reserving sharp rebukes for him—there wasn't any talk of eliminating Gandhi. Instead, other methods to demonstrate dislike were adopted: Savarkar and the Hindu Mahasabha boycotted the Mahatma's Quit India Movement, throwing themselves open to criticism that they were supporting the British reign. The Hindu Mahasabha had, in any case, more important things to worry about than find ways to do away with the Mahatma. Despite its belligerent positioning and support among the Hindu sections of the society, it was not able to make a mark electorally. The Hindu voter may have been glad to have the Mahasabha around to promote its cause or be a neutralizer to perceived Muslim bullying, but he wasn't willing to go to the extent of voting for the organization in parliamentary and Assembly elections. But perhaps there are other explanatory layers to the electoral debacle. The Congress was dominated by tall leaders from the Hindu community who commanded public support. Thus, the party garnered the majority of Hindu votes on the strength of these leaders and a section of the Muslim votes, and sailed through. On the other hand, the Mahasabha nominees were left with a truncated Hindu voter base and nothing by way of non-Hindu votes; its victory in elections was an impossibility. Besides, some important leaders left the organization, leaving it weaker. Syama Prasad Mookerjee, for instance, quit to head the newly formed Bharatiya Jana Sangh;

and Hedgewar, who was with the Hindu Sabha, drifted and went on to found the RSS. If the Hindu Mahasabha remained alive despite these setbacks, it was entirely on account of Savarkar's energetic leadership and razor-sharp intellectual discourse—not to mention his ability to polarise society in ways that helped his and his organization's cause of Hindutva.

SAVARKAR: THE HINDU ATHEIST

Descriptions of Savarkar are fraught with confusion. Let's sample a few. 'His political philosophy had the elements of utilitarianism, rationalism and positivism';[6] 'Savarkar was also an atheist and a staunch rationalist who disapproved of orthodox beliefs in all religions';[7] 'What their (Muslims and Christians) place would be in Savarkar's Hindu Rashtra was not made explicitly clear, but the best they could hope for was a sort of second-class citizenship in which they could live in India only on sufferance.'[8] Was Savarkar an agnostic or an atheist? For the two terms are very different. If he was an atheist and a rationalist (in the way we understand it today), what explains his dependence on the many ancient Hindu texts to create his 'Hindu First' narrative, including a definite emphasis on the phrase, 'punyabhoomi'? Further, was he an uncompromising freedom-fighter or did he capitulate to the British in seeking clemency when he was incarcerated at Andaman & Nicobar? These seeming contradictions have added to his cult image. If

[6]'Vinayak Damodar Savarkar's Strategic Agnosticism: A Compilation of His Socio-Political Philosophy and Worldview'; Siegfried O Wolf; *Heidelberg Papers in South Asian and Comparative Politics* (51), 2010
[7]'Savarkar, Modi's Mentor: The Man Who Thought Gandhi a Sissy'; *The Economist*, December 20, 2014
[8]*Why I Am a Hindu*, Shashi Tharoor, 2018

he was an utilitarian, he should then be in the good company of the likes of John Stuart Mill and Peter Singer—certainly nothing to ashamed of! As a positivist, he would have endorsed the theory floated by the philosopher Auguste Comte that society functions according to a set of general laws, much like the physical world operates on the basis of gravity and other such absolute laws. Comte took the explanation further to expand positivity into a Religion of Humanity.[9]

Savarkar was a revolutionary from his student days, earning the title 'Veer' at the age of 12. Story has it that he led fellow students to face a mob of Muslims that had attacked his village near Nashik, in today's Maharashtra. He later wrote a flattering account of the 1857 revolt, otherwise considered as India's first war of independence, which angered the British enough to ban the work. He was arrested for his association with India House, a British-based group that promoted nationalist feelings and freedom from British rule. Interestingly, India House served as an inspiration for both Communists and Hindu nationalists. He tried to escape from his arrest in Marseilles—the arrest had led to a spat between the British authorities who nabbed him and the French who protested the move as legally unsound because procedures had not been followed—but the attempt was foiled. As a result, he was sentenced to two life-terms (amounting to fifty years in total) in prison on various charges and moved to the infamous Cellular Jail in the Andaman & Nicobar Islands. But he was let off after a decade, in 1921, after he signed a plea for clemency and promised to renounce all revolutionary activities. This act has been held against Savarkar as an example of his sissiness—a charge which

---

[9]Auguste Comte founded the Religion of Humanity as a 'secular' order, which influenced societies in the West.

Savarkar levelled against Gandhi for his pro-Muslim stance. It is true that Savarkar compromised with the British to the extent that he gave such an undertaking, '...I have publicly avowed my faith in and readiness to stand by the side of orderly and constitutional development,'[10] and that he had made at least a couple of similar attempts previously to secure his release but had failed to convince the British authorities to grant him relief. But the bigger issue is: Did he keep his promise to the colonial rulers? Historical material indicates he did not. On the contrary, he went about his aggressive pro-Hindu/anti-Muslim/anti-British activities with greater vigour. While he wrote his much-quoted work on Hindutva as a jail inmate, as a free man he proceeded to spread the message of Hindutva across the country, eventually becoming the Hindu Mahasabha's national president. His supporters are, therefore, inclined to view the clemency plea as a ploy and not as him bowing to the British.[11]

The Cellular Jail episode became a subject of controversy in more recent times. The Atal Bihari Vajpayee regime had installed a plaque in Savarkar's memory near the eternal flame in the jail premises, which was removed in 2004 after the Vajpayee government's exit, on instructions from senior Congress leader and Minister Mani Shankar Aiyar. However, the Congress could do nothing but fume when Savarkar's portrait was unveiled in the Central Hall of Parliament during the NDA rule in February 2003,[12] by then President A.P.J. Abdul Kalam. A few parties, including the Leftists, had written to Kalam to

---

[10]'Savarkar's Mercy Petition'; A.G. Noorani; *Frontline* 22 (7), 2005
[11]In *Veer Savarkar Vindicated: A Reply to a Marxist Calumny*, author J.D. Joglekar draws a comparison with Chhatrapati Shivaji's letter to Aurangzeb during his arrest in Agra, and holds that these were tactical tricks.
[12]thehindu.com, February 27, 2003

keep away from the event to 'preserve the highest secular traditions of the country as enshrined in our Constitution.'[13] Congress president Sonia Gandhi had absented herself from the function. A little over a decade later, Narendra Modi became only the second Prime Minister after Vajpayee to pay homage to Savarkar in Parliament on the latter's birth anniversary in 2014.[14] Incidentally, Aiyar had defended the decision to remove the Savarkar plaque on the ground that he 'personally' believed Savarkar's credentials were suspect over his alleged involvement in Gandhi's assassination. Savarkar had by then become a former president of the Hindu Mahasabha, having quit the post in 1943, and was rounded up by the police as a suspect in the killing. Charged with murder, conspiracy to murder and abetment to murder, he issued a statement, which is part of the official records connected with Mahatma Gandhi's assassination, where he denied any association with the crime and presented robust arguments in his defence. He even produced a telegram through which he had congratulated Mahatma Gandhi on his 75th birthday and wished for god to 'grant him long life and vigorous health'.[15] Savarkar was eventually acquitted. Realizing the history of legality involved, the UPA Government had taken the stand that it had nothing to do with the removal of the plaque, since the plaque had been installed by a foundation set up by a public sector oil company. This was a weak defence; after all, the oil firm came within the purview of the petroleum ministry (headed by Aiyar) and the removal of the commemorative plaque could not have been done by the Minister in his personal capacity. What the incident did was to

---

[13]telegraphindia.com, May 29, 2014

[14]ibid

[15]Retrievable on savarkar.org

further elevate the Hindu nationalist freedom-fighter's image among the Right-wingers.

While the dramatic moments in Savarkar's life and those that happened with relation to him after his death are colourful enough, his enduring contribution—call it pro-Hindu or anti-Muslim, though the first does not necessarily have to lead to the second—is the body of work he has left behind. Nearly all of it has been represented in the book, *Hindu Rashtra Darshan*, neatly arranged into three parts: the first is titled, 'Hindu Pad-Padashahi'; the second, 'Hindu Rashtra Darshan'; and the third is named, 'Essentials of Hindutva'.[16] The first section deals primarily with the affairs of Maharashtra and how various rulers, the chief among them being Shivaji, created situations that favoured the Hindus who had been under the threat of relegation to the sidelines. The second comprises Savarkar's speeches at various sessions of the Hindu Mahasabha from 1937 to 1942. The third is perhaps the most contentious as it has become a sort of calling card for this remarkable Hindu nationalist, not least because it is here that Savarkar undertakes to define Hindu, Hinduism and Hindutva—and draw out nuanced differences among them. It is here that he sets out to establish—for good or for the worse—his belief that Hinduism is but one element of the larger Hindutva concept and that Hindutva, therefore, is the dominant force. It may be recalled that Golwalkar, despite his intellectual strength, had given up on defining the term 'Hindu', saying that like culture, it can only be felt and not explained in words. True, Golwalkar had the advantage of Savarkar's stellar efforts before him, but he chose to play safe. It is for this reason that we must refer

---

[16]*Hindu Rashtra Darshan*; Veer (Vinayak Damodar) Savarkar; Abhishek Publications, 2012

to Sarvankar's 'Essentials of Hindutva' more than Golwalkar's *Bunch of Thoughts* to get an insight on the subject.

But before we do that, it would be worthwhile to return in some detail to the conditions that helped the Hindu Mahasabha gain a foothold, because in them lies the reason for the outfit's—and its most prominent leader, Savarkar's—later popularity. After the Morley-Minto Reforms, which offered a separate electorate for Muslims, the Lucknow Pact of 1916 took the matter forward with the Congress's help. Author Prabhu Bapu wrote, 'The moderate Congress formally conceded separate electorates to Muslims as the basis of new constitutional arrangements after having consistently opposed them since 1909... The pact provided that one-third of the elected members in the central legislature should be Muslims elected by separate electorates... The Congress viewed the pact as a "reasonable price" to pay for Muslim cooperation in the larger goal of securing self-government in India.'[17] The Hindu Mahasabha was not amused by what it called 'surrender' by the Congress at the expense of Hindu interests.[18] In fact, some of the Mahasabha leaders were extreme in the expression of their disgust. B.S. Moonje suggested, 'Leave the Muslims alone,' so that they might 'realise their folly, and in dejection...throw themselves at our feet.'[19] He was also apprehensive of the possibility that Mahatma Gandhi might persuade the Congress to concede even further to the Muslims, something that the Mahatma had hinted at, when he once remarked, 'As a Congressman and as a Hindu, I say that I wish to give the Muslims what they want... I wish to leave

---

[17]*Hindu Mahasabha in Colonial North India,1915-1930: Constructing Nation and History*; Prabhu Bapu; Routledge, 2012-13
[18]ibid
[19]ibid

everything to the honour of the Muslims.'[20] A delegation of the Hindu Mahasabha met Gandhi and told him in no uncertain terms that the organization would oppose him vehemently if concessions were given to the Muslims. But Prabhu Bapu also offered a citation that the Mahasabha was hardly in a position to effectively challenge the Congress. 'The party's narrow social base and its uneven organizational speed in geographical terms challenged its claim to be principal representative of the Hindus in the country.' Nonetheless, the issue did help the Hindu Mahasabha to embellish its credentials of protecting Hindu interests, which it said stood endangered through both Muslim aggression and the Congress's soft-approach.

HINDUTVA'S OFFICIAL DEBUT

Given this situation, it was not enough for Savarkar to maintain an incessant chatter on Hindu faith and Hindu pride; he had to introduce something more attractive to bind the community. That glue was Hindutva, until then neither identified nor explained. For it to stand out, he had to lay down its uniqueness from the other terms used in connection with Hindu thought. 'Hindutva is not a word but a history. Not only the spiritual or religious history of our people, as at times it is mistaken to be by being confounded with that other cognate term, Hinduism, but a history in full.'[21] He then proceeded to reverse a general belief: 'Hinduism is only a derivative, a fraction, a part of Hindutva. Unless it is made clear what is meant by the latter, the first

---

[20]ibid
[21]'Hindutva is Different from Hinduism', Essentials of Hindutva, *Hindu Rashtra Darshan*, Veer Savarkar, 2012

remains unintelligible and vague.'[22] Savarkar had a problem with 'ism' because he believed it referred to a 'theory or a code more or less based in spiritual or religious dogma or system.'[23] He warned against seeking to understand Hindutva from the prism of a code or dogma, and said the nearest in meaning to it would be 'Hindu-ness' and not Hinduism. But whether Hinduism or Hindu-ness or Hindutva, they all derive from the word 'Hindu', and so Savarkar took upon the onerous responsibility—though he was not the first to do so—to decipher the meaning of Hindu. 'Thus Hindu would be the name that this land and the people that inhabited it bore from time so immemorial that even the Vedic name Sindhu is but a later and secondary form of it. If the epithet Sindhu dates its antiquity in the glimmering twilight of History, then the word Hindu dates its antiquity from a period so remoter than the first that even mythology fails to penetrate—to trace it—to its source.'[24] Therefore, he concluded, Hindus are 'all one and a nation'.[25]

But this analysis as a standalone would have been problematic, because then Savarkar would have had to admit that non-Hindus who have been part of this nation for centuries should also be considered part of the cultural ethos of the country. Therefore, he identified three qualifications a person must possess in order to be a Hindu. The first was that this 'land that extends from Sindhu to Sindhu is his pitrabhoomi (fatherland) or matrubhoomi (motherland)'—in other words, he must associate with the Hindu 'Dharam' of this land. The second qualification

---

[22]ibid

[23]ibid

[24]'What is Hindu?', Essentials of Hindutva, *Hindu Rashtra Darshan*, Veer Savarkar, 2012

[25]'Hindus All One and a Nation', Essentials of Hindutva, *Hindu Rashtra Darshan*, Veer Savarkar, 2012

is that he must be a descendant of Hindu parents and claim to 'have the blood of ancient Sindhus and the race that sprang from them in his veins.' And the third criterion, perhaps the decisive one, was that a Hindu must acknowledge this nation, this Sindhustan, as his 'punyabhoomi'—his holy land.[26] This was clever, because it instantly de-recognized anyone outside of a faith that originated in India, as a Hindu or an insider. 'That is why in the case of some of our Mohammedan or Christian countrymen who had originally been forcibly converted to non-Hindu religions and who consequently have inherited along with Hindus, a common fatherland and greater part of the wealth of common culture—language, law, customs, folklore and history—are not and cannot be recognized as Hindus. For though to them Hindustan is pitrabhu as to any other Hindu, yet it is not to them a punyabhu. Their holy land is far off in Arabia or Palestine.'[27] Lest he be accused of thus demeaning the non-Hindus, or perhaps because he wanted to clinch the argument in a logical way, Savarkar added, 'We are not condemning nor are we lamenting. We are simply telling facts as they stand. We have tried to determine the essentials of Hindutva and in doing so we have discovered that the Bohras and such other Mohammedan or Christian communities possess all the essential qualifications of Hindutva but one, and that is that they do not look upon India as their holy land.'[28]

Savarkar was more accommodative of Indian-origin religions such as those of the Sikhs, Buddhists and the Jains, given that they meet his parameters of pitrabhoomi and punyabhoomi.

[26]'Who is a Hindu', Essentials of Hindutva, *Hindu Rashtra Darshan*, Veer Savarkar, 2012
[27]ibid
[28]ibid

He gushed with praise for these co-religionists—'To the millions of our Sikh brethren, their Hindutva is self-evident... The Guru Granth Sahib is read by the Sanatanis as well as by the Sikhs as a sacred word; both of them have fairs and festivals in common.'[29] He called the Sikhs a 'sister Hindu community' and stated, '...the protest that is at times raised by some leaders of our Sikh brotherhood against their being classed as Hindus would never have been heard if the term Hinduism was not allowed to get identical with Sanatanism.'[30] He claimed that the Sikhs were Hindus in the Hindutva sense and not in the sense of religion. 'Religiously they are Sikhs as Jains are Jains, Lingayats are Lingayats, Vaishnavas are Vaishnavas; but all of us racially and nationally and culturally are a polity and a people, one and indivisible, most fitly and from times immemorial called Hindus.'[31] While the Buddhists too, in Savarkar's definition, are part of the Hindutva fold, he had words of caution for them. 'The Buddhists as individuals had nothing to fear from India— the land of toleration—but they should give up all dreams of endangering the national life of India and her independence.'[32] He, however, had nothing but praise for the Buddhist faith, which propagated the 'law of righteousness',[33] and for Buddha— 'I, the humblest of the humble mankind can dare to approach thee, O Tathagat! with no other offering but my utter humility and my utter emptiness... But while thy words are gathered

---

[29]'Hindus in Sindh', Essentials of Hindutva, *Hindu Rashtra Darshan*, Veer Savarkar, 2012
[30]ibid
[31]ibid
[32]'Buddhism, a Universal Religion' and 'Then Came a Reaction', Essentials of Hindutva, *Hindu Rashtra Darshan*, Veer Savarkar, 2012
[33]'Buddhism, a Universal Religion', Essentials of Hindutva, *Hindu Rashtra Darshan*, Veer Savarkar, 2012

from the lips of gods, mine are and my understandings are trained to the accents and the din of this matter-of-fact world.'[34]

Despite Savarkar's attempts to settle the Hinduism-Hindutva issue almost a century ago, controversy on the subject continues to rage. His solutions have actually become fuel to the fire. In addition, there is now a new debate on Hindu nationalism. Who is a Hindu nationalist? Members of the 'secular' Congress party would be loath to be called that, even if they are Hindus. On the other hand, those of the RSS and other Right-wing parties would proudly proclaim themselves to be so. Western media often refers to Narendra Modi as a Hindu nationalist and the BJP as a Hindu nationalist party. It was Bruce D. Graham who popularized the term and said that the Hindu nationalist must not be confused with a Hindu traditionalist. 'Whereas the Hindu traditionalists were conservative in their approach, enlisting time-honoured values to justify the continuation of a hierarchical social order, the Hindu nationalists wanted to remould Hindu society along corporatist lines and to fashion the state accordingly.'[35] Thus, for Savarkar, Hindu nationalism represented power, status and unity for Hindus—and he saw nothing communal in the approach. This opinion is not shared by many academics, especially the Left-liberals. Historian Bipan Chandra, for instance, differentiates between nationalism based on religion and that premised on communal discord. By his yardstick, Savarkar, and the RSS, would be communal rather than Hindu nationalists.[36] Further, since the Hindus comprise an overwhelming majority in India, the Hindu nationalism idea

---

[34]'Reverence to Buddha', Essentials of Hindutva, *Hindu Rashtra Darshan*, Veer Savarkar, 2012

[35]*Hindu Nationalism and Indian Politics*; Bruce D Graham; Cambridge University Press, 1990

[36]*Communalism in Modern India*; Bipan Chandra; Har Anand Publications, 2008

has degenerated into—or strengthened—a majoritarian narrative that on purpose excludes large sections of Indians.

Savarkar, like Golwalkar, had ample time and occasion to expand and refine his philosophies. There were others who could have contributed as much if not more to the Hinduism-Hindutva cause but for the paucity of time. One such figure is Syama Prasad Mookerjee, the founder-chief of the Bharatiya Jana Sangh which, in its later form as the Bharatiya Janata Party, would spearhead, as a political organization, the Ram temple movement in Ayodhya—which has become a metaphor for modern Hindu revivalism.

EIGHT

New Voice, New Party

I would ask you to fulfil in an abundant measure your obligation
for the revival of the glory of Hindu culture and civilization, not
from a narrow bigoted point of view but for strengthening
the very root of nationalism in this country.

SYAMA PRASAD MOOKERJEE

O rdinarily, Syama Prasad Mookerjee would not figure high in the pantheon of Hindu nationalists/ Hindutva champions. Unlike Golwalkar or Savarkar, he does not have to his credit any ideological tract. His stature notwithstanding, he was essentially a provincial leader. Mookerjee wasn't a spiritual guru either, in the mould of Swami Vivekananda or Sri Aurobindo. His political career does not compare in depth with that of Tilak. Yet, he cannot be brushed aside. Let us remember that he had been a member of the Congress party, had headed the Akhil Bharatiya Hindu Mahasabha, was founder-president of the Bharatiya Jana Sangh, and had been an important member of Nehru's first Cabinet. Perhaps no public figure from that time could boast of such an imposing résumé. His entire politics centred on fighting a system that he found prejudiced against Hindu interests. He fought his battles single-handedly, though he had sympathisers for his cause both within the Congress and outside. Had he lived longer and helmed the Jana Sangh for a greater period of time—he was only 52 years of age when he passed away under mysterious circumstances, a closure to which case has not happened to this day—his imprint on the agenda of Hindu nationalism would have been even more momentous. Arguably the crowning glory of his decade-long active politics was his resignation from the Nehru government in protest against the unfair deal the Hindus living in the then East Pakistan had been saddled with, as a result of the Nehru-Liaquat pact. Mookerjee, therefore, deserves to be considered as a towering part of the larger Hindutva construct.

Mookerjee had an excellent academic record before he tentatively got into politics in 1929. He had topped the university examinations in Bengal, been admitted to the 'Indian Bar' of the Calcutta High Court, and studied law at Lincoln's Inn. Like many of his time, he had been drawn to the Congress party and was elected to the Bengal Legislative Council from the University constituency on the party's ticket. But he quit soon after, over differences with the Congress, and contested and won as an independent. 'The party which evoked my sympathy and support was the Congress. The Congress, however, lamentably betrayed the interests of the Hindus... In Bengal, it did not allow a coalition ministry and thereby greatly strengthened the Muslim League and in fact consolidated it.'[1] For close to a decade thereafter, he concentrated on his role as an educationist, in which he excelled by all accounts. The turning point came in 1939 when he came in close touch with Vinayak Damodar Savarkar. 'Dr Mookerjee toured in different parts of Bengal in September 1939 and was greatly perturbed at the helpless position of Bengal Hindus whom the Congress

---

[1] *The Life and Times of Dr Syama Prasad Mookerjee: A Complete Biography*; Tathagata Roy; Prabhat Prakashan, 2012

failed to rouse and protect. While touring eastern Bengal he realised how desperate the position of Hindus had become and how the spirit of resistance against an outrageously communal aggression was dying out—slowly but surely. This was how Dr Mookerjee along with some others...were drawn to Savarkar's influence that gradually took root.'[2] In his presidential address to the Mahasabha in 1938 at Nagpur, Savarkar had given a clarion call for Hindu organizations to reject the Congress and vote for Hindu nationalists. 'The Hindu Mahasabha was compelled to take up the Congress's foolish challenge to the Hindu community and the Mahasabha by seeking to divest the latter of all power to represent the Hindus. The Congressmen, mostly Hindus, drew men, money and vote from the Hindus... but once elected, they called Hindu organizations communal and reprehensibly betrayed Hindu interests while dancing attendance on the Muslim League.'[3] Mookerjee found the observation especially relevant in the context of Bengal. When Savarkar formally relaunched in March 1939 the Mahasabha's caste consolidation programme in the State, Mookerjee was in the forefront to support it. The Mahasabha's event 'coincided with the introduction of the Calcutta Municipal Bill in the Bengal Assembly which gave separate electorates and increased seats to Muslims,'[4] and which further fueled anger among the Hindu population.

The Hindu Mahasabha had found an able leader in Mookerjee to take its agenda forward in Bengal. His credentials were further strengthened when he presided over a 'huge Hindu

---

[2]*Syama Prasad Mookerjee and Indian Politics*; Prashanto Kumar Chatterji; Foundation Books, Revised Edition, 2015
[3]ibid
[4]ibid

conference' held in the State, in which leader after Hindu leader lamented the 'atrocities' on the Hindus and 'anti-Hindu, rabidly communal politics of the Haq-Muslim League ministry.'[5] It was during Savarkar's visit to Bengal in mid-1939 that the thought to join the Hindu Mahasabha got ingrained in Mookerjee's mind. 'Dr Mookerjee, who was deeply impressed by Savarkar's analysis of the Indian political situation and his gospel of unalloyed nationalism to checkmate the anti-Indian policies of the League and the "cowardly passivity" of the Congress, was pressed to join the Mahasabha by Nirmal Chatterjee, S.N. Banerjee, Asutosh Lahiri and others.'[6] Nirmal Chatterjee was the father of Somnath Chatterjee, who later went on to become a leading communist leader and Speaker of the Lok Sabha.

Mookerjee's entry into the Hindu Mahasabha marked the beginning of his rapid rise in Indian politics. His pro-Hindu and anti-appeasement positions became stronger as he rose in stature. Many prominent national leaders were impressed by his work and commitment to the Hindu cause, especially given the prevailing political situation. Among them was Mahatma Gandhi, who told the fired-up young leader: 'Somebody was needed lead the Hindus after Malaviya (Madan Mohan Malaviya)... Patel (Vallabhbhai Patel) is a Congressman with a Hindu mind, you be a Hindu Sabhaite with a Congress mind.'[7] Whether Mookerjee had any longer a Congress mind, is debatable, but he certainly was a committed Hindu Mahasabha leader. This was evident in his quip to the Mahatma: 'But then you will dub me as communal!'[8] Gandhi's response was

---

[5] *The Life and Times of Dr Syama Prasad Mookerjee: A Complete Biography*, Tathagata Roy, 2012

[6] ibid

[7] ibid

[8] ibid

interesting—he said that 'somebody must be there to drink the poison of Indian politics,'[9] drawing an analogy with the story of Shiva, who swallowed the poison that had been thrown up in the Great Churning of the sea. This was as unequivocal an endorsement as any.

Academics had by then taken a backseat in Mookerjee's scheme of things as he plunged headlong into the politics of freedom from British rule and justice for the Hindus. If the Congress was alarmed at the traction the Mahasabha was gaining, the British were equally worried. The Viceroy, who happened to be in Calcutta (during the Hindu Mahasabha's conference in December 1939), 'told London that the Hindu Mahasabha was gradually emerging, and with considerable vigour, as something approaching a political force,'[10] adding that he would 'not be surprised if the Mahasabha were to succeed in stealing a certain amount of Congress thunder.'[11] It is thus not surprising that the British preferred to deal with the Congress with which it could have leverage, and that was possible if the Mahasabha's influenced could be contained. 'Any nationalist consolidation was bound to be disliked by the British.'[12] But the British posed just one of the many challenges for Mookerjee when he began to reorganize the Mahasabha. There was the Muslim League too, which had witnessed to its dismay the growing consolidation of Hindu forces to take its communal agenda head-on. That did not end Mookerjee's and the Mahasabha's problems, though. 'They had further to meet resistance from three important

---

[9]ibid

[10]*Syama Prasad Mookerjee and Indian Politics*, Prashant Kumar Chatterji, 2010

[11]ibid

[12]*The Life and Times of Dr Syama Prasad Mookerjee: A Complete Biography*, Tathagata Roy, 2012

elements within the Hindu community'[13]—the Congress, the Communist Party of India, and a section of the scheduled Castes. Mookerjee noted in his diary that Sarat Chandra Bose (Subhas Chandra Bose's brother) had, in a friendly way, warned Mookerjee against setting up a rival organization in Bengal and said such a body would be met by force.[14] The Communists spewed venom against the Mahasabha, calling it communal, but had no problems in dealing with the Muslim League—which was as communal as the word 'communal' gets. The third opposition was from certain members of the Scheduled Castes who had benefited from the Poona Pact[15] and were being provoked into demanding a separate political space for themselves as opposed to the larger Hindu interests. He began to tackle these obstacles with added determination when he was appointed the working president of the Hindu Mahasabha early in 1940—a precursor to his taking over as the Mahasabha's president from Savarkar, a couple of years down the line. By many accounts, he had begun to succeed. His entry had 'galvanised the Bengal Hindu Mahasabha into a dynamic organization that started to attract the Hindu intelligentsia and began to be looked upon as a force in the Bengal politics. His bold but rational presentation of Mahasabha ideology and his frontal attack on the Congress policy of appeasement of, and comprise with, the Muslim League at the cost of the Hindus created a stir all over Bengal and India.'[16]

---

[13]ibid

[14]ibid

[15]The Poona Pact was an understanding reached between Mahatma Gandhi and B.R. Ambedkar in 1932, which provided for reservation to Schedules Caste members in legislatures.

[16]*The Life and Times of Dr Syama Prasad Mookerjee: A Complete Biography*, Tathagata Roy, 2012

The Mahasabha had also begun to gain from other circumstances. The Second World War had broken out and the Congress was ambivalent over supporting the British in its war efforts. It tried to leverage the situation and gain some kind of commitment from the imperial rulers for independence. That wasn't forthcoming. The Congress's dilemma was seized by the Mahasabha to drive home its point about the national party's confused state of mind and the consequent inability to protect Hindu interests. The Mahasabha's campaign got a further shot in the arm when the Muslim League in 1940 passed a resolution in favour of the creation of Pakistan, which would be a Muslim country. Now was the right time for Mookerjee to press ahead with the Hindu consolidation programme. With the Congress adamant and the Communists declared rivals, the Mahasabha's hopes on uniting the Hindus rested on its ability to convince the Scheduled Castes to remain firmly behind the rest of their Hindu brethren and not succumb to policies that divided the Hindu community. Mookerjee also worked with the Santhal community in the state to persuade them to consider themselves as part of the Hindu fold. All these efforts were being taken in order to ensure that a caste census would then throw up numbers which favoured the Hindus.[17] That would be one way to end the misery of Bengal Hindus 'who were being systematically humiliated and despoiled by the Muslim League with the connivance of the British for the great sin of patriotism.'[18] He felt duty-bound as the state chief of the Mahasabha to deliver to the Hindus what he had promised. The initiatives he took when the Dacca (now Dhaka) communal violence erupted in 1941 embellished his credentials. Although

---

[17]ibid

[18]*Syama Prasad Mookerjee and Indian Politics*, Prashant Kumar Chatterji, 2010

the Hindus living there had managed to counter the Muslim violence, it was clear that several Muslim leaders had instigated the violence against the Hindus. He visited Dacca and 'went directly to the palace of the Nawab of Dacca, the president of the Bengal Muslim League, from where the entire carnage was being planned and operated.'[19] Since Press censorship was in place, he got in touch with Congress president Maulana Abul Kalam Azad and requested him to ask the Congress legislators to support his move for an adjournment motion in the House on the issue. Not getting a response from Maulana Azad, Mookerjee wrote to Mahatma Gandhi, and after the latter's intervention the Congress gave the necessary instruction to its legislators.[20]

THE MOOKERJEE PHENOMENON

Mookerjee's espousal of the Hindu cause in the context of the prevailing socio-political environment, brought him at loggerheads with many influential leaders—including Subhas Chandra Bose and the charismatic revolutionary's brother Sarat Chandra Bose, both of whom were then with the Congress. The Calcutta corporation elections were to be held in March 1940[21] and Netaji Bose, smarting from the humiliation of having to quit the Congress's national presidency following a tiff with Mahatma Gandhi, after having won the contest, was keen to demonstrate his popularity in Bengal. In a bid to prevent the division of Hindu votes and also show the combined strength of the community, Mookerjee suggested that Bose's group and

---

[19]ibid
[20]ibid
[21]*The Life and Times of Dr Syama Prasad Mookerjee: A Complete Biography*, Tathagata Roy, 2012

the Mahasabha work together in the election to checkmate the Muslim League; the official Congress faction was too weak to stand up to the confrontation. Netaji accepted the idea and there was agreement on all seats except two. Bose insisted on his candidate, and 'one night after a long and heated discussion, Sarat Bose broke the joint front.'[22] Left to fight alone, Mookerjee's Mahasabha did well, winning 'about fifty per cent of the seats and gaining tremendous prestige.'[23] In the process, his party had had to face threats from the Bose faction.[24] 'Subhas decided to intimidate and demoralise the Mahasabha candidates by using force. He had his strongmen break all Mahasabha meetings.'[25] However, Mookerjee behaved like a statesman after victory and reached out to Netaji Bose to ensure that together they could chose a joint candidate as the Mayor. Bose spurned his offer and instead struck a deal with the Muslim League and helped install a League candidate.[26] Mookerjee, too, could have arrived at an agreement with the League, but he refused to gain short-term political advantage at the cost of his principles. These bitternesses and conflicts apart, Mookerjee had great regard for Netaji Bose's nationalist drive. The fact that Bose had Leftist leanings did not bother the Hindu Mahasabha leader much, because at least the revolutionary was not a communist! Besides, Bose was more of a socialist, and for Hindu nationalists this was not a big disadvantage; socialists were tolerated, but not the Marxists. Also, according to one of Bose's biographers, Leonard Abraham Gordon, 'Subhas issued no public statements on religion, but Hinduism was an essential

[22]ibid
[23]ibid
[24]*Syama Prasad Mookerjee and Indian Politics*, Prashant Kumar Chatterji, 2010
[25]ibid
[26]ibid

part of his Indianness.'[27] While incarcerated in the then Burma, Bose had written to his sister-in-law: 'Who knows how long we shall have to be in prison? But all our suffering will be bearable if we get the the chance of worshipping the Mother once a year. In Durga, we see Mother, Motherland and the Universe all in one.'[28] This brief digression into an aspect of Subhas Chandra Bose's tumultuous life should reset propaganda about him, especially of the kind circulated by the Communists in order to own him today; and explain why, despite having sharp political differences, Mookerjee was personally close to Netaji.

Bengal was important for the Hindu Mahasabha. It was the only province where the Muslim League dominated, and this domination would have been on an even larger larger scale but for the presence of the Mahasabha and Mookerjee. Bengal was also the only region where the Mahasabha had attained a level of electoral success, having even shared governance with another outfit, the Krishak Praja Party which contained some members who had earlier been with the Muslim League, to deny power to the League in 1941. Such were the local arrangements that Mookerjee had been experimenting with to cut the League down to size. Ironically, it was not just the Muslim organization which fought against the move; the Congress, too, indirectly helped the Leaguers by undermining Mookerjee's and the Mahasabha's efforts. Mookerjee was part of the coalition ministry for barely a year; he quit the provincial regime in protest against the crackdown on Quit India activists, and later immersed himself in relief work after the great famine that struck Bengal. He squarely blamed the Muslim League's regime (which had by

---

[27]*Brothers against the Raj: A Biography of Indian Nationalists Sarat and Subhas Chandra Bose*; Leonard A. Gordon; Columbia University Press, 1990
[28]ibid

then returned to govern the province) and the British for mishandling the calamity.[29]

Besides, his responsibilities had grown. He had taken over as the Hindu Mahasabha's national president, and he must have realized the difficulty of stepping into Savarkar's shoes. Even as he was settling down, Bengal was struck by the worst communal pogrom till date, sharply underlining the apprehensions that he and the Mahasabha had voiced over the years: That of militant Islam seeking to subjugate the Hindu population in the province through violent means. There are various accounts of the incident, but most agree that the Hindus were at the receiving end of a series of well-planned assaults. Various academics and commentators blamed the Muslim League and its goons for the massacres.[30] The provincial government of Huseyn Shaheed Suhrawardy failed to tackle the situation effectively. The tragic incident of August 1946 has gone down in history as the Great Calcutta Killing, as a result of Jinnah's call to observe Direct Action Day and demonstrate the power of Muslim unity. Trouble had been brewing since before, and Mookerjee was aware of it. But 'he just did not have the support of most of the Hindus... Unlike the Muslims who were almost all solidly behind the rabidly communal League (113 out of 119 Muslim seats), the bulk of the Hindus supported the Congress which would never and did never take their side, even in the face of the grossest injustices perpetrated by the League government. A much smaller number supported the Mahasabha which was politically

[29]*The Life and Times of Dr Syama Prasad Mookerjee: A Complete Biography*, Tathagata Roy, 2012

[30]'A City Feeding on Itself', Debjani Sengupta, 2006; '1946: The Making of the Modern World', Victor Sebestyn, 2014; 'Jinnah of Pakistan', Stanley Wolpert, 1984

quite weak in spite of Dr Mookerjee's leadership.'[31] There are widely fluctuating accounts of the number of casualties in the nearly week-long violence that engulfed Bengal, with figures ranging from a few hundred to tens of thousands. According to a report given by Bengal Governor Fredrick Burrows to his superior, 4,000 people had died while 100,000 had been rendered homeless.[32] This was followed by similar horrors in Noakhali and Tippera. The Muslim League laid the blame at the Congress's doorsteps, claiming that the Congress had engineered the violent unrest in order to show the League in bad light and weaken its resolve for Pakistan.[33] But Mookerjee was not to be taken in by such expressions of innocence. The incidents had shaken him enough to bring him to the conclusion that the Hindus would remain unsafe so long as Bengal was not divided. 'Make Suhrawardy (I hate to utter his name) know that…neither he nor his vicious lieutenants can terrorise the Hindus. We should not cease fighting so long as Bengal is not partitioned and the Leaguers are kicked out from the homeland of the Hindus.'[34] His distaste for the Communists was deepened after they were seen to have backed the Direct Action. 'The Communist Party of India openly supported this call to "Direct Action". In their seminal work on the collaboration of the Communists with the Muslim League in pre-independence India, titled "Sickle and the Crescent", Sunanda Sanyal and Soumya Basu have shown the extent to which this collaboration went…communist leaders

---

[31]*The Life and Times of Dr Syama Prasad Mookerjee: A Complete Biography*, Tathagata Roy, 2012

[32]There are media reports of Fredrick Burrows having written to the Indian Viceroy, informing him of the situation.

[33]*The Sole Spokesman: Jinnah, the Muslim League and the Demand for Pakistan*; Ayesha Jalal; Cambridge University Press, 1994

[34]*Syama Prasad Mookerjee and Indian Politics*, Prashant Kumar Chatterji, 2010

threatened jute mill workers and local shopkeepers with dire consequences if they did not join the hartal on Direct Action Day.'[35]

The aftermath of Direct Action Day mayhem was that several hundred Hindu families suddenly found themselves in no-man's land. The men had been made to consume beef, the women had been abducted or raped, and forced conversions had taken place across Bengal. Orthodox Hindu leaders refused to entertain such 'defiled' people. 'When told (by rescuers such as Sucheta Kripalani and Ashoka Gupta) that they had come to protect them, they would say with immeasurable sadness and resignation that it was no use, they were no longer Hindus, no Hindu would drink water touched by them.'[36] Mookerjee realized that this state of affairs could not continue and that the Hindus had to be accepted back if the larger goal of Hindu unity was to be achieved. It made no sense for the Hindus to be thus divided and then expect that their voice would be heard with seriousness. But the task was not easy; he was dealing with a social custom with deep roots. Mookerjee reached out to the Ramkrishna Mission,[37] which agreed to publish a booklet on why such Hindus who were forcibly fed beef or converted or had their modesty violated, should not be ostracized or considered unfit for the Hindu order. Various scholars of Sanskrit and religious gurus too were roped in by Mookerjee to fight the bias. It was, considering the social circumstances of the time, a brave initiative and added to his credentials as a Hindu nationalist. While he was outspoken, the Congress was

---

[35]*The Life and Times of Dr Syama Prasad Mookerjee: A Complete Biography*, Tathagata Roy, 2012
[36]ibid
[37]ibid

guarded and the Muslim League unapologetic. But what of Mahatma Gandhi, who visited Noakhali after the riots in a bid to calm down communal tempers? His belief in the goodness of human beings, even those who had participated in the killings of Hindus, remained unshaken. 'He was once sitting on the floor of a hut in the midst of Muslims and discoursing on the beauties of non-violence. Sucheta Kripalani passed him a note saying that the man on his right had killed a number of Hindus. The Mahatma smiled and went on speaking. In the village of Palla, on January 27, 1947, he was asked: "What should a woman do if she is attacked? Should she commit suicide?" His prescription was in the affirmative. Not one word about bringing the guilty to book. Instead, he was advising rape victims to kill themselves.'[38] Mookerjee had no sympathy for the lofty considerations of the Mahatma, though he was willing to work with the Muslims in a peaceful environment. Months before the carnage, he had written: 'If Hindus and Muslims unitedly try to maintain Indian culture and traditions, and live side by side according to their own beliefs, then there should be no problem. But if Muslims show overmuch of devotion to their own religion and try to dominate the Hindus, then should the Hindus not think how they can defend themselves? The Hindu-Muslim problem will not be solved without a civil war—but if the other side prepare themselves (sic) for it, and we do not do so, we shall lose the war.'[39] The Calcutta and Noakhali killings and the failure of the Hindu Mahasabha to gain electorally had pained him. But there were at least some

---

[38]ibid. The author quotes American journalist Louis Fischer, who had accompanied Gandhi to Noakhali.
[39]ibid. The author quotes from Mookerjee's diary entry dated January 10, 1946, written in Bengali.

silver linings: The British had decided to move out, and India would be free. Mookerjee had never favoured partition, but recent experiences had changed his mind. At least the Muslim Leaguers, led by Jinnah, would be gone!

Mookerjee would have been happier had Sardar Patel become independent India's first prime minister, but that was not to be. Although Patel had been favoured by the majority of the Congress party units from across the country, Mahatma Gandhi endorsed Nehru; thereafter, Patel gracefully accepted the decision and joined Nehru's Cabinet as his deputy. As a Hindu Mahasabha leader, and even earlier, Mookerjee had deep admiration for the Iron Man of India and saw in him the ideal leader that an India where Hindus had respect and protection ought to have. But he was content that at least, by his presence, Patel would be a good counter to Nehru and his misplaced sense of secularism. Besides, Mookerjee felt a sense of satisfaction that by having played a significant role in the division of Bengal, he had denied Jinnah all of the state—and retained Calcutta for India. He was now ready for yet another—though short—innings: That of a Union minister. It must be said to Nehru's credit that he inducted a person who had been openly opposed to his policies and ideology, though it is possible that Gandhi nudged Nehru into doing so. Whatever the case may be, Mookerjee assumed the challenge with confidence, but not forgetting for a moment that he had to continue protecting legitimate Hindu interests when the need arose. The occasion to test his commitment came soon.

NATIONAL AMBITIONS

The country had been partitioned, and so had Bengal. The part of the state under Pakistani control came to be known as

East Pakistan, and it comprised a good number of Hindus. 'At the time of partition, Hindus, including Buddhists, numbered over 13.5 million in East Bengal, owned nearly 80 per cent of its national wealth, organized and financed 95 per cent of its educational institutions.'[40] While West Pakistan had 'been well-nigh cleared of Hindus following a virtual exchange of population, the Hindus of East Bengal failed see the writing on the wall and were also taken in by assurances of Congress leaders like Gandhi and Patel.'[41] Mookerjee had been keeping a sharp watch on the situation of the Hindus in the part of Bengal that had gone to Pakistan, and was less than happy over reports, that had been filtering in, of their plight. 'About 20 lakh Hindus were forced to leave their home in East Bengal during the first two years of Pakistan's existence... But the worst came early in 1950, when a planned massacre of Hindus on a wide scale was started by Muslims all over East Bengal with the direct connivance of the Pakistan government. According to government figures, more than 50,000 Hindus were slaughtered and thousands of Hindu women were abducted and raped.'[42] Demand for strong action against Pakistan grew in India, and Mookerjee especially was extremely agitated. There were suggestions that the Indian Government ask its Pakistani counterpart for an exchange of population—get the Hindus in the affected areas of Pakistan to India[43] and, until then, get an assurance of safety from the Pakistani establishment. Mookerjee sought immediate and tangible action against the atrocity on thousands of defenceless Hindus in Pakistan. Nehru too was upset, but

---

[40]ibid

[41]ibid

[42]ibid

[43]ibid

he expressed helplessness: 'It is obvious that we cannot control the happenings in East Bengal except by consultation with the central government of Pakistan and the government of East Bengal.'[44] So, Nehru got in touch with his Pakistani counterpart Liaquat Ali Khan and the two agreed on a deal, the so-called Nehru-Liaquat Pact. Nehru, as always, had hoped the other side would be as sincere in letter and spirit as he was. But those like Mookerjee shared no such illusion, especially when the Pakistani regime's complicity in the killings was clear as daylight. He had confronted the Prime Minister on learning of the latter's move to reach an agreement with the Pakistani Premier, but Nehru had bluntly told him that his mind had been made up. Unable to digest Nehru's decision, Mookerjee tendered his resignation in 1950. There were others who were equally upset, though they did not quit. In his book, *The God Who Failed*, author Madhav Godbole wrote, 'Vallabhbhai Patel was very critical of the agreement but refrained from resigning in protest.' A year earlier, Mookerjee had also effectively quit the Mahasabha. He was a parliamentarian but belonged to no organization. Now, as a former Union minister, Mookerjee was a leader without a party but full of desire to continue with his agenda of protecting the Hindu cause, strengthening nationalist sentiments, and striking a blow to the policy of appeasement of the minorities.

Mookerjee and RSS chief Golwalkar met soon after the former had quit the Nehru Cabinet.[45] Assorted other persons, both in politics and outside it, also conferred with Mookerjee—this included Hanuman Prasad Poddar, whom we have encountered in an earlier chapter. Meanwhile, Sardar Patel passed away in

---

[44]ibid

[45]*Syama Prasad Mookerjee and Indian Politics*, Prashant Kumar Chatterji, 2010

December 1950, and Mookerjee lost all hopes in the possibility of the Congress heeding Hindu interests any more. Nehru now had no opposition within the party or the government and his brand of Nehruvian secularism became the order of the day. Mookerjee must have believed that there could be no further delay in launching a party to take on the Congress. More discussions followed and the RSS decided to depute experienced people to help Mookerjee shape up the alternative. Besides, there were discussions about drawing in people from the Hindu Mahasabha too. A group of leaders eventually gathered in January 1951 in New Delhi and decided on the name of the proposed party: Bharatiya Jana Sangh.[46] It was decided to not use the term 'Hindu' as it had the potential of kicking up a controversy at the very start. But everyone, including Mookerjee naturally, emphasised that the party should stand by the commitment of a Hindu Rashtra. Mookerjee had also seen the limited impact parties such as the Hindu Mahasabha had had in containing the Congress because of the former's absence on a pan-India basis. While it was strong in some regions, in many others it simply didn't exist. The second decision thus taken was to quickly expand the Bharatiya Jana Sangh across the length and breadth of the country. Once the party came into being, a letter was shot off to the Election Commission seeking recognition. Balraj Madhok[47] played a major role in not just drafting the letter to the poll panel but also in drawing

---

[46]ibid

[47]Balraj Madhok was a mercurial but brilliant politician and Right-wing ideologue who served as the Jana Sangh's chief in 1966-67. However, he was later sidelined due to his sharp differences with Atal Bihar Vajpayee, who was the rising star of the party. Those interested in details can refer to *The Untold Vajpayee: Politician and Paradox*; Ullekh NP; Penguin Viking; 2017.

up the new party's manifesto.[48] Mookerjee was chosen as the party's first president. In his presidential address, he spoke of 'manifestation of dictatorship in Congress rule' and gave an assurance of 'full protection' to 'all classes of people who are truly loyal to their motherland'. Although he avoided of talking about 'Hindu interests', he did state: 'Our party believes that the future of Bharat lies in the proper appreciation and application of Bharatiya Sanskriti and Maryada.'[49] The development did not go unnoticed in Congress circles. Nehru himself chose to respond to Mookerjee, telling him that he would 'crush your Jana Sangh.' Mookerjee retorted that he would 'crush this crushing mentality of yours.'[50]

Mookerjee became a larger than life figure after the mysterious circumstances surrounding his death in Jammu and Kashmir. He had been a critic of a government rule that prevented people from the rest of India from entering the state without a 'permit', and said that since the accession of Jammu and Kashmir had been 100 per cent complete,[51] such rules were incongruous. But his trip to Jammu was not so much to defy the ban but to 'solely acquaint myself with what exactly happened there and the present state of affairs.'[52] A satyagraha movement was on in the state against Article 370, and Mookerjee expressed readiness to meet the Sheikh in case the latter so desired to discuss matters. He was opposed to the Sheikh's policy of appeasement of one section of the community and dislike for the other, whose members had ruled the state before it became

---

[48]*The Life and Times of Dr Syama Prasad Mookerjee: A Complete Biography*, Tathagata Roy, 2012
[49]ibid
[50]ibid
[51]ibid
[52]ibid

part of the Indian Union. As soon as he entered the state's territory after crossing over from Pathankot, the Jammu and Kashmir police accosted him. He was taken to a small cottage situated near the Dal Lake and placed under arrest; it was here that he spent the last forty days of his life. Barely a fortnight after the arrest, Nehru visited Srinagar but avoided checking up on his former Cabinet colleague, who had by then developed several health problems.[53] Mookerjee died on 23 June 1953, and allegations have remained that the state agencies had been deliberately negligent in attending to his medical needs. He had led the Jana Sangh's thrust against any special considerations for Jammu and Kashmir, such as a separate Constitution, separate flag and separate laws. In light of Abdullah's declaration in early 1952 that Kashmir was a 'hundred per cent sovereign body', Mookerjee told Nehru that he would back the Sheikh only if the latter accepted the sovereignty of the Indian Parliament.[54]

While this is not the place to expand into details of the progress of the Jana Sangh, the fact remains that the party struggled to make a mark in elections in the initial years. In the 1952 Lok Sabha poll, it won just three of the 94 seats it contested, with a three per cent vote share; in 1957, it fought on 130 parliamentary seats and succeeded in four; in 1962, it contested 196 seats and won in 14, though with a vote share of only around six per cent.[55] Things changed for the better somewhat in 1967, when the Jana Sangh won 35 seats with a 9.31 vote share.[56] The party had also begun to be noticed as a result of some successes in different states. The Jana Sangh's

[53]ibid

[54]*Hindu Nationalism: A Reader*; Edited by Christophe Jaffrelot; Permanent Black; Sixth Impression 2017

[55]shodhganga.inflibnit.ac.in

[56]ibid

excruciatingly slow march was, among other things, due to the strong hold that the Nehru-led Congress had on the people. Déspite his skirmishes with heavyweights like Sardar Patel, Purushottam Das Tandon, B.R. Ambedkar and Rajendra Prasad, Nehru remained firmly in control and retained his mass appeal. He ceded no space to rival parties. After the 1962 humiliation at China's hands, both the Congress and Nehru personally suffered a loss of image and the Jana Sangh could gain some public attention. But before the Sangh could hold on to it, Nehru died and a fresh wave of public support for the Congress dashed the rival's hopes. The Congress gained yet again when, tragically, Lal Bahadur Shastri died in office too. It was in the initial years of Indira Gandhi, when she was battling a concerted attempt from within the Congress to undermine her leadership, that the Jana Sangh saw a chance. Unfortunately for it, Indira Gandhi outsmarted her opponents and took firm control of the Congress and the country's political system as well. Therefore, the Jana Sangh languished first under Nehru's commanding presence and later under Indira Gandhi's populism. The real change in fortune came after the Jana Sangh transformed into the Bharatiya Janata Party in 1980 (although a rump Jana Sangh remained in existence), and the BJP began to gain ground after a few false starts. While Vajpayee emerged as the unquestioned superstar of the party, it was his lieutenant Lal Krishna Advani who was to emerge as the new Hindutva icon and dramatically rewrite the Bharatiya Janata Party's agenda. But before that, there was another figure that expanded on the ideological base established by Mookerjee and took the Hindutva agenda forward, if in a relatively soft way. He was Deendayal Upadhyay.

NINE

Poles Apart, Yet Similar in Thought

There is a piece of me that likes to fondly imagine my maverick and rebellious nature. But, more accurately, I like to have a nice and cosy institution that I can rub up against a little bit.

— DOUGLAS ADAMS

As we have seen, powerful individuals set the agenda at the all the high points of the Hindu Identity/Hindutva journey, barring the Vedic period, when no predominant single leader or preacher emerged. From Adi Shankaracharya to Ramanuja, from Kabir to Tulsidas, from Vivekananda to Tilak, from Savarkar to Mookerjee, from Hedgewar to Golwalkar, personalities shaped ideologies. There were organizations too—the RSS, the Hindu Mahasabha and the Jana Sangh. But they were also moulded according to the missionary zeal of their guides, on whose charisma they depended to exert influence. Over the years, some like the RSS and the Jana Sangh acquired an internal momentum which kept them not just going, but also growing. Others like the Mahasabha fizzled out with the departure of their icons and became a refuge for ideological renegades with little base or appeal. Perhaps the Jana Sangh too would not have flourished in the manner it did in the decades after Mookerjee, had not the RSS hand-held it and promoted it vigorously for what it was—its political arm. The party had a series of presidents in the post-Mookerjee period whose contributions have been nothing much to write about, until Deendayal Upadhyay took over. The only other instance before his tenure when the Jana Sangh had a prominent face was when Balraj Madhok assumed charge. While every Jana Sanghi was inherently a Hindu nationalist in the sense of the Right definition—a patriotic Indian—Upadhyay additionally formulated his own sub-ideology, Integral Humanism.[1] That became his calling card, and to this date he is remembered for his emphasis on the socio-political and the moral, on the basic principle that every sensitive policy must yield dividends to the last man in the queue and that human values ought to be the core of any political philosophy. It is possible that Upadhyay's imprint would have been deeper in the written history of the Jana Sangh and the Hindutva movement, had he had more time. His tenure was cut short by untimely death—he fell off a train.[2] It would be a little over a decade after this when the Jana Sangh would metamorphose into the BJP, triggering a new chapter in Indian politics. Nevertheless, Upadhyay's contributions preceded his taking over the reins of the Jana Sangh, and he remains an important figure in the larger Hindu Identity story.

---

[1]Integral Humanism became the Jana Sangh's official philosophy. It was a thought that sought to find a middle ground between Marxist socialism and capitalism. Interestingly, Upadhyay believed that this concept adhered to the Advait philosophy enunciated by Adi Shankaracharya. Like Mahatma Gandhi, he felt that religions and moral values had a major role to play in politics and that the Hindu values that had been around eternally, ought to be preserved.
[2]The circumstances surrounding his death remain a mystery. The most widely circulated explanation is that he was pushed out of a running train on the Patna-Lucknow sector by robbers. But his associates such as Nanaji Deshmukh and Balraj Madhok maintained that he had been assassinated by rivals. In recent months, senior BJP leader Subramanian Swamy urged the Prime Minister to order a fresh probe into Upadhyay's death. Even the Congress and members of Upadhyay's family have sought an investigation.

It can be easy to miss out on Upadhyay's role in taking the Hindutva story forward, because he was not given to rabble-rousing; nor did he keep himself in the news with controversial or outrageous statements. But he was one of the few politicians who had grasped the larger context of a 'Hindu Nation', which stood in contrast to 'Hindu Rule.' In fact, for many Hindu Rashtra zealots, the two terms were, erroneously, synonymous. Upadhyay set about correcting the perception and articulating his thoughts in that direction. His intellectual mindset had been shaped by an early exposure to the RSS ideology. He, in fact, abandoned his post-graduation studies to devote himself full-time to the RSS, which he had joined in 1937.[3] He was active in the United Provinces region and was quick to gain recognition in the Sangh for his excellent performance. He eventually became the chief of the region—the first non-Maharashtrian RSS leader then to assume charge of an entire province.[4] In an article Babasaheb Apte wrote for The Organiser in March 1968, he said that Upadhyay's discourse reflected the pure thought-current of the Sangh.[5] It was Upadhyay who was entrusted with the important task of launching the RSS's Hindi publication, *Panchjanya*—a vehicle that would take the Sangh's voice far and wide across the country to the Hindi-reading masses. Recognizing his intellect, the RSS later asked him to formulate a doctrine for the Jana Sangh—an organization which, until Integral Humanism came into being, had been content with political agendas and plans of action as its literature. Before he took over as party president in 1967, he had acquired vast organizational experience, having been the Jana Sangh's general

[3]*Hindu Nationalism: A Reader*, Ed. Christophe Jaffrelot, 2007
[4]ibid
[5]ibid

secretary from 1953 until the year he took over as president.[6] He had devised original ways to explain the complicated. For instance, he said that while many elements go into the formation of a nation, the cultural direction the nation adopts depends on 'Chiti' or nature. It's a term that is virtually impossible to accurately translate into English, but those associated with Indian-ness would understand it well, and will appreciate what Upadhyay noted, 'Whatever is in accordance with Chiti, is included in culture.'[7] He presented the example of Ramayana: Ram defeated Ravan after invading Lanka and installed the latter's brother Vibhishan to the throne. But Ram is not derided for the invasion; instead, he is praised. Similarly, Vibhishan is not condemned for turning against his brother. On the other hand, Ravan, who was a Bhakt and fought bravely, is clearly the villain. 'Why so? The reason behind this is not political. If there is any standard for determining the merits and demerits of a particular action, it is this Chiti; from nature whatever is in accordance with Chiti is approved and added on to culture... Whatever is against Chiti is discarded as perversion, undesirable, to be avoided.'[8]

DEENDAYAL UPADHYAY: A GENTLE HINDU

While Upadhyay formulated a doctrine that was all-encompassing, he did not lose sight of the basic ideals on which the Sangh was formed and that which was derived from its association with the RSS, which was to promote the cause of Hindutva and Hindu Identity. He was effusive in his praise for

---

[6]ibid
[7]ibid
[8]ibid

RSS founder Hedgewar, calling him a 'born patriot'[9] who was determined to oust the British from India by using whatever means necessary. Endorsing the founder's drive to create an organization which would promote the ideals of Hindutva, he said, 'Hedgewar did not initiate a reform movement. The reformists think that through their efforts at institutional changes, man and society can be reformed. To an extent they may be right, and in certain cases they can claim success too. But Hedgewar believed that society needed an "organization" which links individual to society, and that unless this connect is established, no amount of reformist zeal or institutional efforts can bring about any real difference.'[10] Hedgewar's approach, to Upadhyay's mind, was an outcome of his optimistic approach to Hindutva. 'He was an optimist and believed in positivity. It is from this belief in positivity that Hedgewar emphasized on Hindutva.'[11] Looking at it, in the context of the non-cooperation movement that had been launched by the Congress to attain freedom, Upadhyay commented that the non-cooperation drive 'had negativity to the extent that it called for the "bahishkar of British products".'[12] Upadhyay was not being critical but merely pointing to the intellectual nuances in the two approaches. He was, on the other hand, unequivocally critical of the Congress's support (at Gandhi's behest) of the Khilafat demand.[13] 'Khilafat

---

[9]*Deendayal Upadhyay: Sampurna Vadmay (Complete Works of Deendayal Upadhyay)*, Volume 10; Prabhat Prakashan, 2016. Translations are mine.

[10]ibid

[11]ibid

[12]ibid

[13]The Khilafat movement was a campaign by Indian Muslims for the preservation of the Caliphate in Turkey in the aftermath of the First World War. The movement got the support of the Congress after Gandhi's nudge. The idea was that the Indian Muslims would cooperate with the Congress party in the freedom struggle in lieu of the support the latter gave to the

was in every way a communal movement which promoted obeisance to a foreign power. It did not integrate the Indian Muslims with the Indian nation; instead, it sought to dent nationalist feelings. It is because of Khilafat that some prominent Muslims decided to migrate to Afghanistan (which, according to them, was an Islamic state) from India.'[14] On the other hand, he found Hinduism/Hindutva as a binding force, and often remarked, 'When we talk of protection of Hinduism, it is not a religion. But "religion" is what it is translated into. Hinduism comprises Vaishnavites, Sikhs, Jains, Shaivites, Lingayats. All of these taken together is Hindu Dharma. All of them may have different "mat, panth"—but the "religion" is the same.' The opinion is on the same lines as that of previous Hindutva leaders such as Savarkar.

Upadhyay held the Congress responsible for provoking the Muslim community in the country to indulge in fissiparous talk. Here too, he was following in the footsteps of Tilak, Malaviya and other 'pro-Hindu' leaders of the Congress, as well as the Congress's critics from the outside, such as the Hindu Mahasabha and the RSS. In doing so, he alleged, 'the Congress had failed to arouse nationalist credentials.'[15] Scathingly, he accused the Congress of making the 'Muslims aware of their strengths and their bargaining power'[16] in the negative sense. He

---

Khilafat agitation. The movement collapsed after Turkish nationalists abolished the Ottoman sultanate and ushered in a secular democracy. As for Hindu-Muslim unity in India as a result of this extraordinary collaboration between Islamic forces and the secular Congress party, the jury is still out.

[14]*Deendayal Upadhyay: Sampurna Vadmay (Complete Works of Deendayal Upadhyay)*, Volume 10, 2016

[15]*Deendayal Upadhyay: Sampurna Vadmay (Complete Works of Deendayal Upadhyay)*, Volume 9, 2016

[16]ibid

was unsparing of the few attempts the Congress made to dispel the impression that it was engaging in minority appeasement. Referring to a Congress parliamentary party's decision to not align with communal forces, he quoted an Urdu couplet:

'Shab ko mai pe li, subah ko tauba kar li
Rind ke rind rahe, haath se jannat na gayi.'[17]

(Had drinks in the evening, said no more, in the morning,
Remained drunk all through, did not let go of pleasure.)

He lamented in 1961 that hopes of Muslim communalism waning after the country's independence and the creation of Pakistan had been belied. 'After partition, it had been assumed that the poison spread by the Muslim League would dissipate. Old Muslim Leaguers, when they joined the Congress, would become nationalists. But a change of cap does not clean up the dirt in the mind. The old Muslim league mindset still remains.'[18] This frustration did not come about in the 1960s; it had been there in Upadhyay's mind since the decade before, when in the years soon after partition the Congress put into motion a series of policies that were perceived to be not just favouring the Muslims but also antagonizing the Hindu community. In 1956, he wrote about Muslim conduct in the backdrop of these developments, 'On matters of religion, the Muslims are more extremist. How relevant this approach is in the era of tolerance, we shall not discuss here; it's enough to state that the dogmatic Muslim cannot impose its views on others. Since the Mughal times, Muslims have developed a habit of imposing their wishes on others. Even to this day, in many cities where Muslims are in a majority, during Muharram, the Hindus are not permitted

---

[17]ibid
[18]ibid

to conduct their kirtan-katha...'[19] His concern over Muslim separatist tendencies extended to Jammu and Kashmir as well, a subject that had deeply engaged the founder-president Syama Prasad Mookerjee and his colleague Balraj Madhok. He was unsparing in his criticism of Sheikh Mohammad Abdullah. 'Sheikh Abdullah is also preaching separatism. He is engrossed in all sorts of anti-national activities. Jammu and Kashmir has become an arena of political conspiracies, anti-nationalism, anti-social elements, and administrative and political corruption on a massive scale. There is just one solution to all this: Abrogate Article 370 and integrate Jammu and Kashmir properly with the Indian Union.'[20]

MADHOK, THE MAVERICK

Deendayal Upadhyay's contribution to the Jana Sangh's growth is remembered with pride by the BJP, though the same cannot be said of one of his colleagues, Balraj Madhok. And yet, Madhok's role had been no less important. His mercurial temperament and scuffles with senior leaders like Vajpayee and Advani proved his undoing—he was sacked from the Jana Sangh when Advani was the president in 1973. Eventually, he withdrew from active politics and used the time he had to rant against his rivals; he often made the RSS, too, the subject of his ire. He was a puritan who disapproved of the Jana Sangh's dilution of ideological positions. Madhok had opposed the Jana Sangh's support to Jayaprakash Narayan's anti-corruption movement,

---

[19]*Deendayal Upadhyay: Sampurna Vadmay (Complete Works of Deendayal Upadhyay)*, Volume 4, 2016
[20]*Deendayal Upadhyay: Sampurna Vadmay (Complete Works of Deendayal Upadhyay)*, Volume 11, 2016

not because he was principally opposed to the cause but because he believed that J.P.'s Left-leaning 'Gandhian socialism' went against the ideals of the Sangh. 'To Madhok's dismay, the RSS was fully supportive of the alliance that the Jana Sangh, under the leadership of Vajpayee and Advani, forged with J.P.'[21] He continued to create one ruckus after another, leading to his suspension from the party. 'Advani once wrote that one of the major problems Vajpayee faced as president was Madhok who he says "continued to oppose him almost at every turn."'[22]

Madhok had problems with not just Vajpayee but also Upadhyay's philosophies, particularly the Integral Humanism concept. At various party meetings, he questioned the idea and said it reeked of communist leader M.N. Roy's thoughts on radical humanism.[23] Roy eventually moved away from communism but the Jana Sangh had internalized the Integral Humanism concept, which to this date is displayed on the BJP's trophy shelf prominently. It can be speculated that Madhok would have had glorious innings in the Jana Sangh, and later the BJP, had he not confronted the Vajpayee-Advani duo and additionally antagonized the RSS. It could not have been the lack of capability that finished off the maverick leader. After all, he had helped draft the Jana Sangh's manifesto, had prepared the letter which was dispatched to the Election Commission of India seeking recognition to the new party, and worked alongside Mookerjee to put the party on its legs. That he was an intellectual remains uncontested. And yet he was sidelined in favour of Vajpayee.

Former ideologue K.N. Govindacharya said that while

---

[21]*The Untold Vajpayee: Politician and Paradox*, Ullekh NP, 2017
[22]ibid
[23]ibid

one of the reasons could be that Vajpayee was a better public speaker and a charismatic figure, that could not have been the only reason. 'Madhok was one of the Jana Sangh's ablest speakers in English, besides being an adroit organizer. It is well documented how he successfully helped build the Jana Sangh's base in Delhi and several parts of north India by shepherding the anti-cow-slaughter agitation and how he handled the Punjabi Suba situation in the mid-1960s... He also got much acclaim as an active politician who contributed immensely to the party's growth in the crucial years between 1962 and 1967, which saw the deaths of two Prime Ministers and a period when India faced two wars, one with Pakistan and another with China.'[24] But none of this came to his help later in his battle with Vajpayee. 'Madhok was furious when Vajpayee was named for the coveted post of the BJS president. He launched a campaign accusing Vajpayee of being sympathetic to the Congress party and to the Left.'[25] His career effectively came to an end the day Advani met RSS chief Golwalkar days before the 1973 Kanpur session of the Jana Sangh and apprised him of the troubles Madhok was causing. Golwalkar asked him to take all the necessary steps to maintain the party's discipline and health, adding that no one—not even a former party president—could be immune from action.'[26] Equipped with this carte blanche, the party sacked Madhok.

But Madhok's Hindutva leanings did not go away. He may have been given forcible retirement from politics but nothing could take away his sharp intellect or his unambiguous stand on contentious issues, which was in contrast to the politically

---

[24]ibid
[25]ibid
[26]ibid

correct positions his former colleagues took. In an interview during the Vajpayee rein, he dismissed the demolition of the Babri mosque as a non-issue: 'According to me, the mosque was a symbol of national shame, a symbol of foreign invasion. A temple was destroyed to build it. So it (the demolition) is no issue at all.'[27] In that interview, he also paid a back-handed compliment to his old rival Vajpayee's handling of the issue. 'He says he is a Nehru-ite, and there is no reason to disbelieve him. But the party that he leads has some elements of Hinduism in it. This dichotomy between the image of the leader and the image of the party is costing the party dear. He cannot be a Nehru-ite and a (Vallabhbhai) Patel-ite at the same time.'[28]

Madhok's puritanism was not always based on personal whims but rooted in ground realities. In one of the many interviews he gave since being shown the door, he said the BJP would do well to not imitate the Congress in ideological positions, merely to gain ground. 'For the BJP to come up and counter the Congress, it has to stick to its basic ideology and not harp on values which the Congress has believed in. The two parties are distinctly different from each other and if there is any confusion within the BJP, it is on account of Vajpayee and Advani who have done greater harm to the Hindu cause than anybody else.'[29] He reminded the interviewer of his role in the formation of the Jana Sangh. 'Both Vajpayee and Advani were nowhere in the picture and even the RSS had no role to play in founding the Jana Sangh.'[30] Madhok's animosity towards Vajpayee goes back to even before the tussle

---

[27] rediff.com, March 18, 2002

[28] ibid

[29] merinews.com, May 6, 2016. The website quotes an interview given to Hindustan Times.

[30] ibid

for power in the Jana Sangh began. 'When I criticised Nehru in the wake of the Chinese aggression, Vajpayee came up to me and told me I would never be elected to the Lok Sabha again. Acharya Kripalani, who was sitting nearby, told me not to take Vajpayee seriously since the latter was Nehru's planted man in the opposition.'[31]

Part of the harangue is easily explained. It is the outburst of a bitter man who believes he was short-changed despite his contributions to the party. It was his unwillingness to change and recognize the changes happening around him, including the rise of younger leaders like Vajpayee and Advani. It was also the failure to keep a check on his acerbic temperament. He had thus many drawbacks, but his role in the promotion of Hindutva is equally significant. Whether it was the 'Muslim question' or the 'Indianised approach' issue, Madhok presented lucid arguments—even if they seemed to many as needlessly alarmist and at times even deliberately inflammatory. In one of his most famous and oft-quoted tracts, he noted, '...The Muslim problem as it has emerged in India today is entirely the creation of the ruling Congress party, particularly its present leadership, which has developed a vested interest in Muslim communalism for Muslim support... Had this leadership learnt the lesson of partition and had it been serious about solving this problem for good, it would have taken concerted steps right from 1947 to wean away the Muslim masses from the communal leadership of the Muslim league... This policy of appeasement of Muslim communalism is reminiscent of a similar Congress policy in pre-partition days, and its disastrous results.'[32] Madhok, interestingly, conceded that the Muslims could have been shaped

---

[31]ibid
[32]*Indianisation? What, Why and How*; Balraj Madhok; S. Chand, 1970

into nationalists. 'It (Congress) could have built up a really patriotic leadership among Muslims and brought them into the national mainstream with little effort. But it did quite the opposite. It systematically worked up in their minds imaginary fear of nationalist parties like the Jana Sangh and tried to keep them tied to the apron strings of the Congress by offering them baits like continuation of polygamy among them and going out of the way to reconstruct Aligarh Muslim University without changing its communal and anti-national character. By doing so, it prevented the modernization of Islam, which is an essential prerequisite for its Indianisation.'[33] The deftness with which Madhok introduced polygamy and AMU as symbols of Muslim separatism is to be noted, more so since both issues have been the subjects of much debate even in today's time.

His agenda of Indianization included an introduction of the Devanagari script for Urdu, a release of Hindu holy sites in Ayodhya and Mathura from the 'hands of Muslims', and the compulsory use of Hindi and other Indian languages at the 'highest state' in education.[34] He also wrote of the need to rewrite history to reflect Indian realities. 'The tampering with history and removal of references to India's traditional heroes and heroines from the textbooks in the name of secularism and eradication of communalism, is most impolitic and may have the opposite effect. Historical memories cannot be effaced by whitewashing history... The proper thing is to let the rising generation know about these things.'[35] He added that the Jana Sangh, 'being the champion of Indian nationalism and committed to preservation and strengthening of Indian unity,

---

[33]ibid
[34]ibid
[35]ibid

feels particularly concerned about this state of affairs.'[36] Madhok may have been marginalized in the Jana Sangh's larger scheme of things, but the party did officially accept his thesis that the Muslims needed to 'Indianise' themselves if they were to be considered as part of the national mainstream, and particularly, 'nationalists.' Indeed, the party, while acknowledging the 'diversities in our national life', emphasized that 'for the promotion of unity and nationalism, feeling for one culture should be imbibed.'[37] Madhok's theory that 'it is wrong to think that anyone who is born in India irrespective of his emotional loyalty and attitude towards the country, ipso facto becomes an Indian in the true sense'[38] continues to resonate today. It needs to be noted here that the term 'Indianisation' was not introduced by Madhok—it had been used earlier by the likes of Sri Aurobindo. The Jana Sangh ideologue did, however, expand upon it considerably and gave it a political edge that served the Jana Sangh and later the BJP well enough, both politically and ideologically.

Two persons could not have been more different than Upadhyay and Madhok were. But they shared a common belief in the positivity of Hindutva and the need to keep it as the core of the Jana Sangh. The BJP rediscovered it in the 1980s, though the consequences, beginning from Ayodhya and spreading elsewhere soon after, were to be tectonic in nature.

---

[36]ibid
[37]shodhganga.inflibnet.ac.in
[38]ibid

TEN

Two Men and One Mission

Wanted: A man who will not lose his individuality in a crowd, a man who has the courage of his convictions, who is not afraid to say 'No' though the world says 'Yes'.

ORISON SWETT MARDEN

In the early 1980s, Hindutva proponents were faced with near extinction. Indira Gandhi had stormed back to power following the disastrous Janata Party experiment. Her grip on the Congress party was iron-like; in any case, her opponents from within had jumped ship three years earlier to team up with the opposition camp and were now in the wilderness, and the Congress was hers to mould and dictate to, as she liked. Although she was known to visit assorted Hindu religious figures and babas of various kinds and had her personal spiritual guru in Dhirendra Brahmachari, she remained a Nehruvian secularist at the core. She was a shrewd politician who understood the benefits of cultivating a pro-minority image. Additionally, her policies and programmes were steeped in populism, which endeared her to the masses, including the majority community, all of whom were by then addicted to doles. Four years before she made her triumphant return, Indira Gandhi had moved to introduce the term 'secularism' in the preamble to the Constitution, further embellishing her secular credentials, especially among the minorities and the Scheduled

Castes. If the Congress was entirely subservient to her, the Left offered only a token resistance—it could not possibly oppose her 'pro-poor' initiatives, the list of which was breathtakingly long. Meanwhile, the Janata Party had disintegrated, partly due to her machinations and partly as a result of ego-clashes among senior leaders of the failed party. The transition of the Jana Sangh to the Bharatiya Janata Party had just happened and so the party was still finding its feet. While the BJP had leaders of national stature such as Atal Bihari Vajpayee, it was still no match for Indira Gandhi's charisma and her popular outreach. Aiming to be the next credible challenger to the Congress, the BJP needed an issue that would catch the people's imagination and also be in line with its principal ideals. The party had realized that anti-Indira Gandhism would not work. In was in this political environment that the BJP's second most powerful leader, Lal Krishna Advani, began to craft a renewed Hindutva campaign—one that promised to both restore Hindu pride and expose the Congress's politics of minority appeasement.

At around the same time, a gentleman by the name of Bal Thackeray had begun to gain traction in Maharashtra, particularly Mumbai (then Bombay). Like Advani, he also took some time to shape a pro-Hindu image. But his beginnings were very different. The Shiv Sena, a party he helped establish, made its debut by targeting the south Indian population for its influence in the city—from the media down to the street hawker level. Later, the antagonism was to be extended to people of north India who had 'failed to assimilate' with the Marathi cultural ethos. The Shiv Sena, under Thackeray's leadership, thereafter metamorphosed from being just pro-Marathi manoos to being pro-Hindu. Thackeray didn't see any real difference between the two: Maharashtra was the land of Chhatrapati

Shivaji, who had ensured that his region did not capitulate to the Mughals. And Maharashtra was also a Hindu crucible—tall Hindu leaders like Savarkar, Hedgewar and Golwalkar came from there. In his own way, Bal Thackeray was shaping up as the Hindu Hriday Samrat (the darling of Hindu hearts). It was only natural that in the years to come, the Shiv Sena would align with the BJP in the political sphere. Advani, on the other hand, was a dyed-in-the-wool Jan Sanghi; all he needed to do was to find a way to redraw the BJP's gameplan to reclaim the diluted, if not lost, Hindutva space. The immediate years after the BJP's formation were not the right time, more so when Vajpayee was the party president. It was only after six years, in 1986, when Advani took over the mantle from Vajpayee, that the BJP's Hindutva thrust began to happen.

ADVANI EMERGES AS HINDUTVA 'HARDLINER'

Vajpayee's reluctance to take a hardline position was understandable. The party had just been formed and it needed to reach out to all sections of society if it were to become an effective challenger to the Congress. It was the time to consolidate and not to ruffle feathers. Besides, Vajpayee had learned through his tussles within the Jana Sangh, particularly with the irrepressible Balraj Madhok,[1] that the best course was to take everybody along through a process of consensus-building. In a party that was known to be hawkish on issues, his was the liberal voice. Vajpayee's image-building was superb, because he did it without actually reneging on the party's core beliefs. His pro-Hindu views were exactly those of his peers, including Advani. In one of his musings many years later as

---

[1] *The Untold Vajpayee: Politician and Paradox*, Ullekh NP, 2016

Prime Minister, he sent out the following statement from his New Year retreat in Goa: 'Secularism is being pitted against Hindutva, under the belief that the two are antithetical to each other. This is incorrect and untenable. Secularism is a concept of the State, enjoining upon it the duty to show respect for all faiths and to practice no discrimination among citizens on the basis of their beliefs. In this sense, India has been secular since the beginning of her known history... Hinduism's acceptance of the diversity of faiths is the central feature of secularism in India.'[2] Vajpayee then went on to slam critics of Hindutva: 'Some people project Hindutva...in a narrow, rigid and extremist manner—an unfortunate and unacceptable interpretation that runs totally contrary to its true spirit.'[3] Further, his thoughts expanded in a way that brought back remarks of the likes of Savarkar and Golwalkar. 'There is no difference between such Hindutva and Bharatiya, since both are expressions of the same thought.'[4] These thoughts are no different from that which Advani professed.

By the time Advani took over the party presidentship, the Vishwa Hindu Parishad had stepped up its campaign for a Ram temple at the spot where the mosque stood in Ayodhya. Hindu mobilization had begun in full force.[5] India's northern belt was in the grip of the Hindutva wave, but politically the pro-Hindutva lobby was still weak. Rajiv Gandhi was two years old as Prime Minister and his sheen was still intact. The opening of the gates of the disputed structure for Hindus to pray at had set the cat among the pigeons. But within two years of Advani

---

[2] rediff.com, December 31, 2002
[3] ibid
[4] ibid
[5] *Hindu Nationalism: A Reader*, Ed. Christophe Jaffrelot, 2007

assuming charge, the situation had changed. Rajiv Gandhi's regime was mired in various allegations of corruption, his trusted minister V.P. Singh had raised the banner of revolt, and many of those whom the Prime Minister had lifted from obscurity to positions of power had left his side. It cannot have been a coincidence that the BJP's decision to join the pro-temple movement formally happened in 1989 when Rajiv Gandhi was at his weakest. The Ram temple became part of the BJP's election manifesto—where it has remained to date. V.P. Singh had no problems with the BJP's position on the temple and its Hindutva when he took the party's support from outside to form the government at the Centre, following an election which saw the Rajiv Gandhi-led Congress party's defeat. The Left parties, which too backed the government from outside, had qualms about the fact that they were supporting a regime which had the backing of the BJP, and that too a BJP led by 'hardliner' Advani.

Meanwhile, the Vishwa Hindu Parishad continued to go about its task, whipping up passions in the name of the Ram temple and against the Babri mosque. It remains a matter of speculation whether Advani would have taken the game-changing decision of embarking on a Rath Yatra from Somnath to Ayodhya, had the V.P. Singh regime not implemented the recommendations of the Mandal Commission to provide reservations to Other Backward Classes.[6] The Yatra's impact

---

[6]On August 7, 1990, Prime Minister V.P. Singh announced in Parliament his government's decision to accept the report of a panel headed by Bindeshwari Prasad Mandal, which recommended 27 per cent reservation to Other Backward Classes in government institutions. The Mandal panel, called the Second Backward Class Commission, had been set up by the Morarji Desai regime in 1979. Mandal submitted his report in end-1980. The Desai regime had fallen by then, and Indira Gandhi and later Rajiv Gandhi kept the report

was such that leading Right ideologue K.N. Govindacharya likened it to Gandhi's Salt March.[7] The Ram Rath Yatra was a political initiative, though with a religious goal in mind. It began with Somnath in Gujarat,[8] and the final destination was Ayodhya. Led by Advani, the procession, covering several states in its journey, mobilized thousands of volunteers from the larger Sangh Parivar and drew in support from ordinary citizens in millions. Advani addressed hundreds of meetings along the way, and the Yatra expectedly raised tempers across the country. In some places, passions led to violence. If V.P. Singh had sought to divide Hindu votes through the Mandal master-stroke and put the BJP at a disadvantage, Advani was out to make sure that the Hindu electorate was aroused sufficiently enough to thwart those designs. Rattled by the Yatra's success, V.P. Singh asked friendly state regimes to put a spoke in the wheels. Lalu Prasad Yadav, then chief minister of Bihar, responded without delay: When Advani's chariot reached the state, the senior BJP leader was taken into custody and restrained from proceeding further. The incident made Lalu Prasad Yadav an instant hero, and to this day he recounts the decision as among his most sterling achievements. Meanwhile, the BJP withdrew support to the V.P. Singh government and the regime fell. The Raja of Manda was to soon become history, but for Advani the political campaign for Hindutva had only just begun to show results. In the 1989 Lok Sabha election, the BJP had secured 85 seats

in a deep freeze. V.P. Singh revived it to supposedly counter the BJP's growing belligerence on the issue of Hindutva.

[7] *Hindu Nationalism: A Reader*, Edited by Christophe Jaffrelot, 2007

[8] The choice of Somnath was symbolic. The famous Shiv temple there had been destroyed by Muslim invaders. After independence, Vallabhbhai pushed successfully for its reconstruction, against the wishes of Jawaharlal Nehru, who gave in after Mahatma Gandhi blessed the reconstruction.

(up from two in the 1984 outing) and played an important role in propping up the V.P. Singh regime. It aimed for a higher number from hereon.

Freed from the fetters of obligation to the V.P. Singh regime, the party decided to go all out. Advani's Hindutva credentials had by now been firmly established and the BJP's roadmap was clear: It would focus on the issue of construction of a Ram temple in place of the Babri mosque. Two years after the Rath Yatra, the mosque would come down, and with it one chapter in the BJP's Hindutva drive would also come to an end. Advani's second term (1993-98) would thus begin in the post-Babri mosque era on a more sombre note. He was to return for a third term as president (2004-06), but before then the BJP had assumed power at the Centre along with its allies, and the temple promise had been confined to the manifesto with no more public agitations. There was a government to be managed, and nearly all of the BJP's allies were uncomfortable with the Hindutva drive. Besides, being the country's Home Minister and Deputy Prime Minister, Advani could not have possibly resumed his Hindutva activist role. Managing mercurial partners like Mamata Banerjee and J Jayalalithaa was a full-time job in itself, in addition to launching a spate of developmental initiatives such as highway construction and resetting the country's foreign policy. Thus Hindutva took a backseat, though it never disappeared from the party's radar. In the aftermath of the mosque's demolition, Advani believed that his Rath Yatra would have gone through without obstacles (and perhaps the V.P. Singh government may have been saved, at least for that moment) but for pulls and pressures within the ruling Janata Dal. 'Left to himself, V.P. Singh may not have obstructed the Rath Yatra of 1990. But the internal politics of the Janata Dal forced his hand. To prove himself a greater patron of the minorities than Mulayam Singh Yadav, V.P. asked Lalu Prasad to take action before the Uttar Pradesh chief minister did so. Lalu did as he was told, and became instrumental in terminating V.P.'s tenure. This time it has been Arjun Singh who has played Mulayam Singh to P.V. Narasimha Rao. The denouement may well be the same.'[9] On the mosque's destruction, Advani offered a quote from Tulsidas: '*Hoi hai soi jo Ram rachi rakha* (That alone happens which Lord Ram wishes to happen).'

BALASAHEB, THE HINDUTVA TIGER, ROARS

Bal Keshav Thackeray, popularly known as Balasaheb Thackeray, was not given to such philosophical soliloquies. His Shiv Sena derived its name from the legendary ruler Chhatrapati Shivaji, and the 'army of Shivaji' believed in action more than in words. Once the Shiv Sena was formed in 1966, it lost no time in going after the South Indians in Mumbai who, according to him, had not just monopolized virtually every major activity in the city but had also pushed the sons of the soil to subordinate positions.[10] The Sena began as a social organization, and it took nearly a decade for Thackeray to register it as a political party, because of fear of the Emergency.[11] But once that was done, the party lost no time in making its presence felt, at last on the streets. It was buoyed by the response it had received at the first meeting it held to announce its arrival. 'Thackeray had not expected a good response to his call to rally... He wanted

[9]*Hindu Nationalism: A Reader*, Ed. Christophe Jaffrelot, 2007
[10]*Hindu Hriday Samrat: How the Shiv Sena Changed Mumbai Forever*; Sujata Anandan; HarperCollins Publishers India, 2014
[11]ibid

a small town hall or a school ground as the venue for the Shiv Sena meeting, just to test the waters.'[12] But he was persuaded to hold it at Shivaji Park, which eventually was overflowing with crowds. The party had indeed arrived. Then came Dussehra day, and the Sena held a massive public meeting, which was to become thereafter an annual affair. The party stepped up its anti-outsiders and pro-Marathi manoos campaign, and slowly but surely managed to create a space for itself. Politically, its opponent was the Congress, though he had done a business of some sort with that party—he had backed the Emergency and later called a bandh to protest against Indira Gandhi's arrest when the Janata Party was in power.[13] Years later, he was to turn his ire to the Muslim population, though he often said he was not against patriotic Muslims, but those who had betrayed the country and resorted to terrorism. 'I am not against the Abdul Hamids, only against the Dawood Ibrahims.'[14] Thackeray also took on human rights activists who had questioned encounter killings of gangsters in Mumbai: 'What about the innocents they (criminals) kill? Have they no right to exist?'[15]

Thackeray began to veer from the sectarian agenda of pro-Marathi manoos to a larger pro-Hindutva construct sometime in the 1970s, though all through that decade he had kept his inclination understated not just because of the Emergency but also due to his admiration for Indira Gandhi. That did not prevent him, though, from conducting experiments off and on to test the waters. One such attempt was made at Durgadi fort in Kalyan, which housed both a temple and a dargah. Because

---

[12]ibid
[13]ibid
[14]ibid
[15]ibid

of communal sensitivity, movement of both the communities had been restricted by the administration. He and his men managed to breach the security there and storm the place.[16] This pleased him to no end, and he decided to make the anti-(unpatriotic) Muslim drive a permanent feature of the Shiv Sena. In 1984, after Indira Gandhi's assassination, Thackeray decided to pull out all stops to take up the Hindutva cause. The BJP had then still not fully latched on to the concept, busy as it was in struggling with its electoral failures. In a by-election meeting in the state in 1987, Thackeray 'made three incendiary speeches inciting Hindus against Muslims.'[17] His candidate won and the matter went to court. The Shiv Sena chief was found guilty of fanning religious feelings to secure votes and was disenfranchised by the court for six years. That was no problem because Thackeray had neither contested an election nor was he inclined to do so in the future. The episode strengthened his pro-Hindutva credentials. Years rolled by and the Shiv Sena grew in stature in Mumbai and the neighbourhood as it maintained its pro-Hindu and 'anti-nationalist Muslims' position. Sixty years after Tilak, the political Hindutva movement had once again arrived in Maharashtra, and Thackeray was its new leader. Everything that the pro-Hindu identity campaign had adopted—from Hindutva to opposition to cow slaughter to insistence on the singing of Vande Mataram to a deep hatred for the Communists—Thackeray had absorbed it all. The Congress had begun to worry, but it tolerated Thackeray's rise because he was a good counter to the Communists whose influence among the mill workers, in particular, was considerable. He was now ready for the next level.

---

[16]ibid
[17]ibid

It is ironical that Maharashtra's Hindutva icon missed out on the most 'glorious' moment for the rabble-rousing Hindutva elements: The destruction of the Babri mosque. By all accounts, the Shiv Sena was absent from the scene, with some of its leaders having been recalled by Thackeray from the site before the structure was razed to the ground. Thackeray would later say that 'if' any Shiv Sena member had been there, he would have personally been very 'proud' of his contribution to the destruction.[18] This miss-out did not in any way dilute his happiness over the mosque's destruction. Thackeray believed that iron-will to stand by one's conviction was often seen as authoritarianism, but he was not averse to being called authoritarian; in fact, he seemed to relish it. He once kicked up a controversy by offering qualified praise to Adolf Hitler: 'The killing of Jews was wrong. But the good part of Hitler was that he was an artist. He had good qualities and bad. I may also have good qualities and bad ones.'[19]

After the Shiv Sena-BJP formed the government in Maharashtra in 1995 and the Sena's candidate became the chief minister, Thackeray said he was the 'remote control' of the chief minister.[20] He compared the spread of the Muslim population in the country to cancer. 'Muslims are spreading like a cancer and should be operated on like a cancer. The country should be saved from the Muslims.'[21] His choice of words created chaos not just among his rivals, but also his sympathizers. For instance, he remarked in an interview that 'Islamic terrorism is growing and Hindu terrorism is the only way to counter it. We

[18]ibid
[19]ibid
[20]*Unfinished Innings: Recollection and Reflections of a Civil Servant*; Madhav Godbole; Orient Blackswan, 1996
[21]*India Today*, June 15, 1984

need suicide bomb squads to protect India and Hindus.' And then, in another interview to a leading national daily, Thackeray stated his wish to see a 'Hindustan for Hindus' and to 'bring Islam in this country down to its knees.'[22] His pro-Hindu image got a further boost when he backed the Kashmiri Pandits who had been driven out of their homeland by extremists in the valley. It must not be forgotten that Thackeray had gathered praise for the manner in which the Shiv Sena had countered the menace of the underworld in the eighties—and since the underworld was seen to be largely controlled by members of the minority community, this tirade seamlessly merged into the Sena's anti-unpatriotic Muslim push.

The Shiv Sena may not have been involved—much to its chagrin—in the destruction of the Babri structure, but it 'rose to the occasion' during the communal riots and terror attacks in Mumbai soon thereafter. There are many versions of the communal riots that broke out in the city in December 1992 and continued over the following month. The Shiv Sena was blamed for the flare-up and the violent incidents, and it was also said that the police did nothing to stop the rampaging mobs. On the other hand, the Sena maintained that it had retaliated to communal attacks that first came from certain Muslims in the wake of the Babri demolition. A commission of inquiry headed by B.N. Srikrishna was set up, but its report was rejected by the Sena-BJP government. The report is said to have laid the major portion of the blame at the Shiv Sena's doorsteps. Interestingly, even the Congress-Nationalist Congress Party government in the state that came later, did not either accept the report or initiate action on the basis of the findings. A few stray cases went to the courts but beyond a few convictions—followed

---

[22]*Indian Express*, January 29, 2007

by grant of bail—of a handful of Shiv Sena leaders, nothing much happened.

In the middle of November 2012, all of Mumbai came to a standstill. Bal Thackeray had passed away and a state funeral was underway at Shivaji Park. According to media reports, it was the first public funeral in the city since that of Tilak in 1920, and an estimated one million people turned up on the streets to pay their last respects to the departed leader. The Tiger was no more, but his unapologetic Hindutva continues to inspire not just the Shiv Sena, now led by his son Uddhav Thackeray, but also Raj Thackeray's Maharashtra Navnirman Sena, which was formed after Raj walked out of the Shiv Sena in end-2005. There are not many politicians who had or have the courage or conviction the senior Thackeray did. Those who call him a paper tiger forget that the mightiest of Mumbaikars went out of their way to be in his good books. The list included not just politicians but also business leaders and prominent film personalities. With a snap of his fingers, he could bring Mumbai to a standstill, and change the fortunes of even those who boasted of high connections. The case of popular actor Sanjay Dutt is a good example. Initially, the Shiv Sena had been opposed to the actor for his alleged involvement in 1993 terror attacks. But after some parleys with Sunil Dutt, who was with the Congress, Thackeray suddenly declared that Sanjay Dutt was innocent and being framed. The entire Sena then rallied behind the beleaguered star. Sanjay Dutt never forgot the favour. On hearing of Thackeray's illness (he had been put on a life-support system), an emotional Dutt rushed to see him, and later said, 'Balasaheb is a father figure to me. He is a great man. He stood by me at a time when no one else came forward to support me... It broke my heart to see him in a critical position.'[23]

The cartoonist-turned-social activist-turned-politician who never contested elections but always held the remote left behind a legacy of Hindutva which inspires his followers and angers his detractors.

---

[23]timesofindia.indiatimes.com, November 16, 2012

ELEVEN

Day of Pride, or of Shame?

You cannot disown what is yours. Flung out,
there is always the return, the reckoning, the
revenge, perhaps the reconciliation.

JEANETTE WINTERSON

Y   ou have to understand, this is a Hindu country.' It was
not an RSS ideologue speaking. Nor was it a rabble-
rouser from the Vishwa Hindu Parishad, or a Bajrang
Dal loose cannon. He was a 'secular' and veteran politician. He
belonged to the Congress. Further, he said this as the country's
Prime Minister, to one of his colleagues, Mani Shankar Aiyar. It
was P.V. Narasimha Rao.[1] Apparently, Rao made the observation
in the context of pressure on him to take pre-emptive measures
against damage to the disputed Babri mosque in Ayodhya. His
reluctance to do so resulted in the demolition of the structure
on December 6, 1992. After the incident, pressure grew on the
government to rebuild the mosque in the exact same place.
Interestingly, according to notes found in Rao's private papers,[2]
yet another secular stalwart and a senior colleague, Sharad Pawar,
cautioned against the move. Pawar said a rebuilt mosque would
be exploited repeatedly to launch mass movements, leaving the

---

[1]*Half-Lion: How P.V. Narasimha Rao Transformed India*; Vinay Sitapati; Viking,
2016
[2]ibid

minority community in a state of fear. After the destruction, Rao dismissed not just the Bharatiya Janata Party government in Uttar Pradesh, but the party's regimes in Madhya Pradesh, Rajasthan and Himachal Pradesh on the ground that the chief ministers of these States were members of the just-banned RSS. Rao's conduct was that of a besieged politician, and not so much as one whose credentials were anti-Hindu. Implicit in both his and Pawar's remarks was an acknowledgement of the dangers of antagonizing the majority religious order.

The then Prime Minister's 'Hindu country' remark could not have been off-the-cuff; Rao was not given to casual conversations—not with someone like Aiyar, with whom he never got along well and was even more measured than he characteristically was. Had he then stated an obvious truth he believed in, despite the fact that the preamble to the Constitution of India refers to the country as 'secular'? Could that remark not have been the outcome of his own grooming at home and in the larger environment in which he grew up? Is it not possible that his own scholarly temperament, which was shaped by his deep study of Hindu sacred texts, made him refuse to take 'anti-Hindu' positions? It may be argued that the protection of the mosque was not an act of anti-Hinduism. But to do so by dismissing a pro-Hindu State regime that stood for a Ram temple at the disputed site, or rounding up potential Right-wing mischief-makers even when no damage had been done, was something Rao's Brahmin body and soul could not digest. But post-demolition, he had been left with no choice. Even so, it was a gamble that could have gone wrong had the courts intervened against the dismissal.

Fortunately for him, the challenge in the Supreme Court fell flat after the court held that the sacking of a state regime for violating secularism was lawful under Article 356.[3] But the dismissal was mostly symbolic, given that Kalyan Singh had put in his papers soon after the event, taking full responsibility, according to media reports of that time, for the development. Politically though, he was not finished, as he contested and won from two Assembly constituencies in Uttar Pradesh in 1993. He was to become the chief minister yet again between 1997 and 1999, during which time he reiterated that a Ram temple would be constructed at the disputed site. His government faced a crisis after the Bahujan Samaj Party, which had backed the BJP regime to shut the doors on the Samajwadi party, withdrew support.

The game was not over. Naresh Agarwal, who was then with the Congress, broke away from his party and along with 21 MLAs extended support to Kalyan Singh and helped him survive. A twist in the tale came when Agarwal and his group later withdrew support, and the government was dismissed by the Governor. A Congress government was then sworn in, post-haste. The story did not end there, though. The matter went to the court, which struck down the Governor's orders, and Kalyan Singh's regime was reinstalled. All through this drama, Kalyan Singh stuck to his pro-temple stance, which further embellished his pro-Hindutva credentials.

The buck, however, stopped with Rao. He had been in touch with a variety of leaders from the BJP, the Vishwa Hindu Parishad, and also with an assorted number of religious figures, and all had assured him that no risk attended to the mosque. 'Rao had personal relations with a number of swamis, from the Sringeri Shankaracharya to the Pejawar Swami. In addition, he deployed the Tamil Nadu Congressman P Kumaramangalam

---

[3]ibid

to reach to the gurus of south India, while his astrologers N.K. Sharma and Chandraswami dealt with north Indian godmen... In each of these meetings, Rao would press for an assurance that the Babri mosque would be unharmed. He would even break into Sanskrit and quote Hindu scriptures to make his point.'[4] His personal reach also extended to leaders of the BJP, especially Vajpayee, with whom he had a good rapport, and the then RSS chief Balasaheb Deoras. 'Most of the RSS leaders were Brahmins. They respected Rao who was also a Brahmin.'[5] He also secretly negotiated with Ashok Singhal, the 'messianic leader' of the RSS.[6] The November of 1992 was used for reaching out to Advani. 'Since Rao's friend Vajpayee was less involved in the Ayodhya movement, Rao focused his attention on L.K. Advani... If anyone could protect the mosque, Rao felt, it was Advani.'[7] But Rao did admit to Aiyar in some frustration three days before the mosque came down that he had tried everything. He could have taken pre-emptive steps then, but he decided to trust Kalyan Singh's assurance that the mosque would not be touched by the karsevaks that were supposed to gather at the site on December 6.

There are differing versions on what the prime minister was doing exactly, as the mosque was being ripped apart by a frenzied mob in Ayodhya. The story that Rao was asleep circulated when a number of senior Congress leaders said they had not been able to reach the Prime Minister over the phone, with his staff telling them that Rao did not 'want to be disturbed'.[8] His biographer Vinay Sitapati wrote: 'That Rao was

---

[4] ibid
[5] ibid
[6] ibid
[7] ibid
[8] ibid

sleeping is verifiably false. From 12.15 pm, when the first dome (of the mosque) was under attack, Rao was on the phone with several of his officials.'[9] Sitapati quotes a senior bureaucrat as saying that the Prime Minister was being informed on a regular basis and that around two in the afternoon, as the mayhem was being played out at the disputed site, Rao had a meeting with senior officials. After the destruction, Rao addressed the nation through a broadcast: 'I would like to say very clearly that we shall no longer suffer the Machiavellian tactics of the communal forces in this country.'[10] The damage to his image and to the Congress had been done by then. The Muslim vote bank began to shift—and it had options in the form of the Samajwadi Party and later the BSP. In neighbouring Bihar, Lalu Prasad Yadav strengthened his 'secular' credentials. In one instant, unfairly, all of Rao's achievements in turning around the Indian economy and reining in the Congress's first family's influence were wiped out. Nor did his path-breaking foreign policy initiatives that came later on, manage to shift public focus from the blot of the demolition of the mosque. Rao had become persona non grata in a party that he had been associated with since his youth days. The fact that the office of the Congress party shut its gates when his mortal remains were to be brought in, on December 24, 2004, has been extensively reported. The party did not forgive him even in his death.

The mosque demolition came as a shock even to a hardliner like Advani (at least in those days he was one). He termed the event as 'one of the most depressing days in my life', and said he had 'seldom felt as dejected and downcast' as he did on that

---

[9]ibid
[10]ibid

fateful day.[11] He provided three reasons,[12] none of which included any desire in favour of the mosque. The first reason was that he believed the incident had 'impaired BJP's and RSS's reputation as organizations capable of enforcing discipline.' The second was that it had reduced to dust 'a meticulously drawn plan of action thereunder the Uttar Pradesh government was steadily marching forward towards discharging its mandate regarding temple-construction, without violating any law or court order.' And the third reason he offered was that the incident would 'affect the BJP's overall image (not electoral prospects) adversely, and to that extent, our cause would suffer a temporary setback.' In fact, Advani was less than apologetic about the Ayodhya movement the Sangh Parivar had launched and said that it was 'slanderous' to say that it was against secularism. 'It is wrong to describe even the demolition of the Babri structure as a negation of secularism. The demolition is more related to lack of a firm commitment in the general masses to the rule of law, and an exasperation with the frustrating sluggishness of the judicial process.'[13] He added that the BJP was 'unequivocally committed to secularism.' He then stated what many Hindu nationalists have consistently maintained—that 'India is secular because it is predominantly Hindu. Theocracy is alien to our history and tradition.'[14] These are the kind of remarks that 'secularists' have pounced upon to reiterate that the RSS and its family members are communal by nature. But, there is some truth to what Advani said. It would be impossible to identify a Muslim nation which is truly democratic or where non-Muslims have equal

---

[11]*Hindu Nationalism: A Reader*, Ed. Christophe Jaffrelot, 2007
[12]ibid. The editor cites an article written by L.K. Advani and published by Indian Express on December 27, 1992.
[13]ibid
[14]ibid

rights of the sort that India provides to its minorities. There would be rare instances, if any, of Hinduization under Hindu kings, but there are many in the case of Muslim rulers such as Aurangzeb or invaders like Mahmud of Ghazni.

The mood in the BJP may have been sombre, but others were celebrating, not bothered with niceties. Vishwa Hindu Parishad, for instance, maintained throughout that the demolition was nothing to be ashamed of. Its leaders even decided to mark 25 years of the incident as Vijay Divas (Victory Day) or Shaurya Divas (Bravery Day), with a view to keeping the momentum on the temple project[15] and ensuring that the dreams of millions of Hindus would be fulfilled once a grand temple came up. The Bajrang Dal, whose members were booked for taking out a procession to mark the 25th anniversary in Ayodhya,[16] has partnered the VHP in realizing the 'dream'. Incidentally, a few BJP leaders have taken positions which, while not celebratory, have also not condemned the mosque's razing to the ground. Senior party leader and now Union Minister, Uma Bharti, is one among them. Along with Advani and Murli Manohar Joshi, she too faces charges of criminal conspiracy in the demolition, and the matter is with the judiciary now. Bharti has likened the Ayodhya campaign to an 'open movement, like the movement against the Emergency.'[17] She debunked any criminal conspiracy angle and pointed out that she was there at the site, as were many others—'Crores of BJP workers, lakhs of officials and thousands of political leaders participated... I don't see any conspiracy.'[18] Like the VHP and the Bajrang Dal, the Shiv Sena

[15]Indusscrolls.com
[16]firstpost.com, December 4, 2017
[17]hindustantimes.com, May 30, 2017
[18]ibid

has never lost sleep over the event that shook the country and had tragic fall outs in Mumbai. 'The demolition was a matter of pride for us. We have never shied away from it. I know that below the mosque, existed a temple... The Muslims who came to India were aggressive and destroyed our temples... Can we keep getting beaten? Can bombs keep getting exploded and we remain silent?'[19]

BJP leaders like Advani viewed the collapse of the mosque as a law and order problem and a breakdown in the discipline of the Right cadres. Opponents of the Sangh Parivar interpreted the development as the definitive exposure of the Sangh's communal, intolerant and divisive agenda. But the underlying sentiment in Thackeray's defiance comes closest to what millions of Hindus could have felt—or were made to feel by those who gained from arousing those sentiments. The story presented was in a nutshell, the following: 'For centuries the Hindus of India, despite being in majority, were subjugated first by Muslim invaders, then by Mughal rulers and later by the British who often pandered to the desires of the Muslim population to keep them divided from the rest of the population and make it easier for the colonial power to govern. The Congress, despite having tall Hindu leaders and flourishing on the votes of the Hindu community, consistently appeased the Muslims before and after independence. It sought to reduce the importance of the likes of Tilak, Rajendra Prasad, Sardar Patel, Malaviya and Mookerjee who spoke up for the Hindus, and it tried to suppress the credibility of the RSS. The Congress had no problem in doing business with the Indian Union Muslim League, but it deemed the Sangh Parivar as communal. Speaking up for the

---

[19]Refer to Bal Thackeray's interview to journalist Rajat Sharma, available on YouTube.

Muslims was considered an act of fostering unity in diversity, but raising issues of the Hindu community was seen as majoritarian brinkmanship.' The mosque's demolition, as far as the avengers were concerned, was, therefore, a metaphor for the triumph of Hindutva after centuries of having been bullied. For them, the final straw that broke the camel's back was the refusal of the Muslim community to respect their religious sentiments—their insistence on a temple at the disputed site because they believed it to be the birthplace of their deity Ram—and instead give primacy to a mosque built by a foreigner.

For the strident anti-Babri mosque lobby, the incident was not merely that of a structure's demolition but the assertion of a Hindutva identity which had been unfairly suppressed. And for them, the movement did not end with Ayodhya; there were Mathura and Varanasi too, where mosques had been constructed during the Mughal rule by the side of important temples. Of course, it would be unfortunate if this lobby were to repeat the Ayodhya mayhem here too or even attempt to do so. At the same time, one must dismiss the argument forwarded by liberals that the existence of a mosque and a temple cheek by jowl was a living example of cultural syncretization. It would have been so, had the two structures come about through a happy consensus between the two communities. Instead, the mosques were constructed next to temples to send across a message of Islamic superiority by the then Muslim rulers.

The pro-temple lobby also claimed that since no namaz was being offered when the structure was locked up by a court order in 1949-1950, it could not even be termed as a mosque. The counter has been provided by one Hashim Kidwai who said that he (as a child) along with his family had, between 1939 and

1941, visited the mosque and offered noon prayers.[20] Koenraad Elst, Right-wing author and probably the only foreigner to have written extensively on the temple-mosque dispute, responded to this claim thus: 'The fact that someone who wants to prove that the place was still in use in 1936-49, merely says that his family went there twice in more than two years, and does not say that he saw with his own eyes that the Muslim community gathered there every Friday, is a strong indication that the place no longer was a community mosque in regular use.'[21] But mosque or not in the strictly religious sense, the structure was certainly a matter of faith for the Muslims, and a prestige issue as well. Once it was razed to the ground, deeply hurt and shocked Muslims were to even wonder if they had done the right thing in staying back in India after partition.[22] In any case, the incident had a tectonic impact: 'It led to the fall of two national governments, the dismissal of four state governments, two electoral victories of the BJP, ultimately leading to its present poster position, riots claiming a few thousands of lives, dozens of temple demolitions from England to Bangladesh, and terrorist attacks, pioneering a now-popular new tactics, viz. many synchronous attacks at different locations within one city, first tried in Mumbai on March 12, 1993. While that seemed to be the closing date of Ayodhya-related violence, the controversy again played a minor role in the next major communal conflagration, the Gujarat riots of 2002. These started with the arson of a train coach

---

[20]koenraadelset.bharatvani.org

[21]ibid

[22]The author of this book was a journalist based in Goa when the Babri mosque came down. He spoke to several prominent Muslims then, and some of them said that they should not have trusted the claim of secularism that a free India promised, and ought to have gone to Pakistan where their mosques, at least, were protected.

carrying Hindu pilgrims from Ayodhya, and helped to make chief minister Narendra Modi the undisputed Hindu leader and today, the prime minister.'[23]

As the national opposition to the Sangh family, the Congress has been the most vocal over the decades in denouncing the BJP and its ilk for promoting communal polarization through the exploitation of the Ram temple issue. The BJP has indeed gained from communal divides, though it alone cannot be blamed for the division. It is understandable why the Congress is keen to restrict the narrative to a period that comprises the run-up to the mosque demolition and the aftermath of the event, and not begin from the beginning. In telling the story from the start, soon after independence, it will have to explain its own role in creating the crisis. In 1949, idols of Hindu deities were found in the mosque. It was said that the idols had been surreptitiously installed by members of the Hindu community to lay claim to the site.[24] 'On the night of December 22-23, 1949, someone broke into the mosque and there installed the idols of Rama and Sita. The following day, thousands of local Hindus assembled and proclaimed this event as a miracle. The chief minister of the United Provinces (today's Uttar Pradesh), G.B. Pant, asked the district magistrate to remove the idols but the man refused to obey—his wife was elected MP from Gonda on a Hindu Mahasabha ticket two years later, and it seems plausible the ploy had been masterminded by activists of this party.'[25] But before the issue could be exploited, Prime Minister Nehru ordered preventive arrests and sealing of the gates of the structure.[26]

---

[23]koenraadelset.blogspot.in
[24]*Half-Lion: How P.V. Narasimha Rao Transformed India*, Vinay Sitapati, 2016
[25]*Hindu Nationalism: A Reader*, Ed. Christophe Jaffrelot, 2007
[26]ibid

Now, devotees could worship the idols only from the outside of the locked gates.[27] This status quo remained in place for the next four decades or so. It is pertinent to note that while the gates were shut, the idols remained in place despite a pro-Hindu chief minister ordering its removal. Even Nehru did not move to get them removed from the mosque. Their continued existence offered a good reason for the Hindu devotees to keep visiting the structure and conducting their prayers from outside—and more important, provided a strong reason for the belligerent Hindutva elements to keep up the pro-temple momentum at the disputed site. In 1986, Prime Minister Rajiv Gandhi ordered the opening of the gates of the disputed structure and thereby allowed Hindu religious activities to be conducted inside. This was an 'error of judgement' and an act of 'absolute perfidy'.[28] He did this not because he had suddenly developed a liking for Hindutva, but because he realized the pitfalls of politically alienating the country's majority community. He was on a 'balancing act' spree, having placated the Muslims (and antagonized the Hindus) by placing a ban on Salman Rushdie's *The Satanic Verses*, and negated a Supreme Court verdict on the Shah Bano case by amending the Constitution. Many years later, a Congress party panel was to present a report to the party's high command, suggesting, in a different context—and obliquely—the need for the party to not anger the majority community, after its debacle in 2014. 'The panel found that fighting the polls on a "secularism versus communalism" plank hurt the Congress that was identified as pro-minority, resulting in substantial electoral gains for the BJP [sic]... The party's minority appeasement policy also proved

---

[27]*Half-Lion: How P.V. Narasimha Rao Transformed India*, Vinay Sitapati, 2016
[28]*The Turbulent Years: 1980 – 1996*; Pranab Mukherjee; Rupa Publications, 2016

counter-productive, the committee submitted.'[29]

Rajiv Gandhi's decision to open the disputed structure's gates had immediate consequences. It energized the Vishwa Hindu Parishad to launch an agitation to 'break free the idols of Rama and Sita from captivity.'[30] 'Sacred' stones began to be ferried from all over the country to the lay the foundation for a grand Ram temple at the site. While the VHP was exhorting the majority community members to say with pride that they were Hindus, Rajiv Gandhi had begun to face the heat over Bofors and other scandals, and his reputation was dipping at an alarming pace. His party eventually lost the Lok Sabha election to V.P. Singh, newly minted as the anti-corruption messiah. Around the same time, a controversial event took place: A foundation stone for the Ram temple was laid at the disputed site, with senior government officials in the know, not just of the incident but also of the fact that the place was disputed.[31]

Despite these machinations, the Congress party lost the elections not just nationally but also in Uttar Pradesh. Mulayam Singh Yadav's newly formed Samajwadi Party emerged the winner and Yadav became the chief minister. Since then, the Samajwadi party has grown into a major player in Uttar Pradesh—and at the central level too, on different occasions. His victory also signaled the end of the Congress hold on the State, a situation which prevails to this day. Meanwhile, the pro-temple juggernaut which had already been unleashed continued to move on. Although it picked up momentum in Rajiv Gandhi's later tenure, the ground was laid earlier, in 1984, when the Vishwa Hindu Parishad helped form the Sri

---

[29]hindustantimes.com, August 17, 2014
[30]firstpost.com, January 29, 2016
[31]ibid

Ramjanmabhoomi Mukti Yagna Samiti, which also coincided with the creation of the Bajrang Dal.[32] The difference between then and 1989 was that in the latter period, the BJP, which had generally kept a distance from the temple campaign, stepped in the arena, as a consequence of L.K. Advani's initiative. 'The party based an important resolution formalizing this shift during the Palampur (Himachal Pradesh) meeting of its national executive in June 1989, when the decision to finalize an alliance with the Mumbai-Maharashtra-centred Hindu party, the Shiv Sena, was also made.'[33] By now, the consequences of the Congress party's confused handling of the issue since the 1950s were becoming clear. Advani's Rath Yatra and the killing of more than a dozen Hindu karsevaks, on orders of firing on a mob by chief minister Mulayam Singh Yadav, happened around the same time frame—October 1990. They were supposedly preparing to storm the mosque in Ayodhya, and Yadav not just defended the firing orders but also took pride in doing so. He said: 'If more people were to be killed for the country's unity and integrity, the security forces would have done it.'[34] It is not clear how the country's integrity and unity had been threatened. In any case, the incident earned him, in pejorative terms, the sobriquet, 'Mullah Mulayam'.

By the time Rao took over as prime minister, it was not 'Mullah Mulayam' he had to deal with in Uttar Pradesh but Kalyan Singh, who was the chief minister and who had been at the forefront of the pro-temple agitation. We have seen how the build-up to the demolition happened and Rao's response to it. In recent weeks, one television news channel apprised viewers

---

[32]*Hindu Nationalism: A Reader*, Ed. Christophe Jaffrelot, 2007
[33]ibid
[34]timesofindia.indiatimes.com, November 22, 2017

that weeks before the demolition, Rao had met Kalyan Singh in New Delhi and informed him that according to archaeological excavators who had spoken to Rao, a temple had indeed existed at the site where the Babri mosque stood.[35] That he did nothing in pursuance of this information, by way of persuading the pro-mosque lobby to soften its position, is a matter of record. Perhaps he believed that the information was not yet definitive, or he felt that nothing catastrophic was around the corner for him to take a position at that stage. Anyway, the issue soon gained traction as a legal tangle, besides being a matter of faith. The establishment of legal rights became a battle of scientific evidence—through excavations by the Archaeological Survey of India, which had commenced before the destruction of the structure but picked momentum after the mosque's demolition. The fight for Hindu assertion began to take a new shape. During the existence of the mosque, the two parties aligned against each other were the Vishwa Hindu Parishad and the Babri Masjid Action Committee, and they were the ones exchanging material with each other to present their respective narrations.

To begin with, both sides relied on literature that had been left behind—academic and religious texts, accounts by travellers who came to India from outside, and the British administration officials. Of these, Austrian Jesuit priest Father Joseph Tieffenthaler's written record was seized upon by the pro-temple lobby to strengthen its case. Although the learned

---

[35]In February 2017, Times Now interviewed Yogendra Narayan, a senior bureaucrat in Uttar Pradesh when Kalyan Singh was chief minister. Narayan revealed the days before the mosque's demolition, Narasimha Rao had summoned Kalyan Singh to Delhi and told him of an ASI report which spoke of the remnants of a temple at the place where the Babri mosque stood. Narayan was not present at the meeting; he had waited outside in the car. Kalyan Singh later informed him of the discussion.

priest, who visited what was then Avadh between 1776 and 1772, was not certain whether the mosque was built during Babur's time or in Aurangzeb's reign, he was sure that it had come upon the ruins of a temple dedicated to Ram. 'Emperor Aurangzeb got the fortress called Ramot demolished and got a Muslim temple, with triple domes, constructed at the same place. Others say it was instructed by Babor.'[36] There are other similar accounts, such as the one by French traveller C Mentelle, which speaks of a temple in Ram's name that had stood at Ayodhya before the mosque came up.[37] The readiness to attribute the destruction of the temple and construction of a mosque to Aurangzeb is possible because the Mughal ruler has gone down in history as fanatically anti-Hindu and responsible for the destruction and desecration of various temples across the regions he ruled. Authors such as Kishore Kunal belong to that category.[38] But while he has produced interesting material to justify his claim, the general academic tilt is towards Babur. In any case, the pro-temple camp is less concerned with the ruler and more focused on their stand that the mosque had been built on the ruins of a Ram temple.

The first scientific evidence came into the public domain sometime in 1988. Professor B.B. Lal, who had served as director-general of the Archaeological Survey of India, hinted, at a seminar in Delhi, at remains of a temple below the Babri mosque.[39] The distinguished archaeologist had undertaken a project involving various sites associated with the epic Ramayana,

---

[36]*Ayodhya Revisited*; Kunal Kishore; Prabhat Prakashan, 2016. The author has reproduced the English version of the traveller's account originally written in Latin, as published in London's *Modern Traveller* in 1828.

[37]ibid

[38]Refer to my article in dailypioneer.com, March 2, 2017

[39]*Rama and Ayodhya*; Meenakshi Jain; Aryan Books International, 2013

and Ayodhya was one of them. He said in the seminar: 'In the Janmabhoomi area, the uppermost levels of a trench that lay immediately to the south of the Babri masjid brought to light a series of brick-built bases which evidently carried pillars thereon. In the construction of the Babri Masjid a few pillars had been used, which may have come from the preceding structure.'[40] Experts such as S.P. Gupta, a former director of Allahabad Museum, wrote later that on the basis of excavations, it could be said that a structure was built at the site in the 11th century, that the structure was built on pillars, and that the structure existed till the very end of the 15th century as the Islamic glazed-ware recovered at the site, could be firmly dated to the 15th-16th centuries.[41] Gupta dismissed the possibility of a Buddhist or Jain structure that may have predated the mosque at the site. Faced with material emanating from professionals who could not be dismissed through rhetoric, the Babri Masjid Action Committee's experts, many of them reputed Left historians, launched a counter-movement to discredit the findings or the interpretations, or both.

The likes of Romila Thapar retorted that merely because the pillar bases were found running behind the wall surrounding the mosque, did not mean that they were beneath the mosque as well.[42] They further claimed that brick pillar bases did not necessarily indicate there was a temple. Neither the bases nor the architecture on the stone pillars were exclusive to Hindu temples, they added. The ball bounced back and forth in the two competing camps. A question was raised on the absence of any reference to the existence of a temple in B.B. Lal's original report. The response to this, by Gupta, was that Lal's mandate then was to determine the antiquity of the site and not the presence of a temple. It would be safe to assume, however, that at some point in time, the pro-temple lobby appeared to have gained the upper hand on the basis of archaeological material, because suddenly the Left historians changed track. One of them, Suraj Bhan, even went to the extent of conceding that there may have been a Hindu structure before, but that it had collapsed by itself between the 11th century and the 16th century.[43] Veering away from the subject and seeking to fortify his position, historian Suraj Bhan slammed Hindu rulers for denying entry into temples to many Hindus—he even took on the practice of Sati![44] More to the point, he said that even if 'hypothetically speaking, a Ram temple were to be found below the Babri Masjid...the wrongs of the past cannot be rectified today.'[45] The issue of the moment was not about rectifying past errors, but establishing whether the mosque had been built over a razed temple. A timely addition to the pro-temple group was K.K. Muhammad, then superintending archaeologist at the Archaeological Survey of India. In an article, he wrote that he had seen the excavated pillars at the site which clearly pointed to the ruins of a temple: 'Ayodhya is as holy to Hindus as Mecca is to Muslims. Muslims should respect the sentiments of millions of their Hindu brethren...'[46] Launching a scathing attack on the Left historians—or JNU historians, as Muhammad calls them—Elst said that many people, including the media, were 'reluctant to face an unpleasant fact: The guilt of its heroes,

---

[43]ibid
[44]ibid
[45]*People's Democracy*, March 3, 1991
[46]*Indian Express*, December 15, 1990

the "eminent historians".'[47]

While historians and assorted academics continued with their spat, political changes were taking place nationally. Rajiv Gandhi was out of office, V.P. Singh was prime minister and he too would be shown the door soon, Chandra Shekhar would come and go—paving the way for Rao to assume prime ministership. Various national and international seminars related to the subject were being held, and both lobbies continued to push forward their respective positions. The BMAC historians continued to dispute the contention that Ayodhya was a sacred spot for Hindus, that a temple dedicated to Ram was ever constructed, that even if a temple existed, it had been pulled down to make way for the Babri mosque. On the other hand, those such as B.B. Lal refuted these claims with the evidence at hand. 'In 1992, a booklet, *Ram Janmabhoomi Ayodhya: New Archaeological Discoveries* (Sharma, Y.D., et al), published for the first time pictures of pillar bases taken at the time of excavations by B.B. Lal…'[48] Now, the Left historians, faced with hard evidence, sought to discredit the findings by claiming that those pillar bases were 'walls'—one historian even claimed it had been part of a cowshed![49]

In the midst of such claims and counter-claims, Rao sought to revive discussions across the table between the two groups in October 1992,[50] barely two months before the mosque was demolished. Nothing came of the effort since the BMAC experts refused to accept the material on the ground that all of those had been planted. Earlier, the Chandra Shekhar regime too had made serious efforts to resolve the issue but failed because the BMAC

[47]'Ignoring the Truth That's Unsettling', Koenraad Elst, dailypioneer.com, January 26, 2016
[48]*Rama and Ayodhya*, Meenakshi Jain, 2013
[49]ibid
[50]ibid

kept shifting the goal post.[51] One month after the demolition, the central government made a Presidential reference to the Supreme Court under Article 143 of the Constitution on the single point: 'Whether a Hindu temple existed or any Hindu religious structure existed prior to the construction of Ram Janmabhoomi-Babri Masjid (including the premises of the inner and outer courtyards of said structure) in the area on which the structure stood?' Nothing came of that either, since a five-judge bench of the apex court refused to give an opinion on the question it was asked. But it did validate the acquisition of land by the Rao government in the aftermath of the demolition, setting aside objection that the Centre's decision had violated the rights (this time of the pro-mosque lobby) given under Article 25 and 28 of the Constitution for religious practice which forms an essential and integral part of the religion.

The most important set of excavations in a bid to settle the issue was done under the Allahabad High Court's directive by the Archaeological Survey of India in 2003—the destruction of the mosque had allowed the excavations to be more elaborate than before, and so a total of 90 trenches were excavated in the entire site. Various technologies such as ground penetrating radar were used. More importantly, the excavations were done under the supervision of a court-appointed team. The ASI submitted its report to the court on September 22, 2003,[52] which, inter alia, said that the structures found 'are indicative of remains which are distinctive features found associated with the temples of north India.'[53] By then, the BMAC had ceased to exist, and

[51]*Ayodhya Revisited*, Kishore Kunal, 2016
[52]*Rama and Ayodhya*, Meenakshi Jain, 2013
[53]ibid. The author quotes from the report—*Ayodhya: 2002-03;* Volume I; ASI 2003

others such as the All India Muslim Personal Law Board and the Sunni Central Wakf Board had got into the act. The report ought to have ended the matter, since it was a result of work conducted under the supervision of an independent authority— the Allahabad High Court. But the Left historians, now having attached themselves to the new parties, were unwilling to let go. They raised doubts on the competence and even motives of the Archaeological Survey of India, with one noted historian, Irfan Habib, writing for a newspaper even before the final report had been submitted, wondering whether the ASI would 'simply set its sights at finding what those in power wish it to find: the remains of a temple.'[54] In other words, the Leftists had already indicted the Rao government, not to speak of ignoring the fact that the excavations had been done under the aegis of a court.

Incidentally, while it is true that the issue had gained traction because the courts failed to settle the dispute over the decades, it is also a fact that there have been many court rulings on limited points relating to the subject, and a full settlement came through the Allahabad High Court verdict in September 2010 parcelling the land among the three parties to the dispute. It gave the area covered by the central dome to Bhagvan Shri Ram Lalla Virajman and others on the ground that it was the 'birthplace of Lord Ram as per faith and belief of the Hindus'; the area within the courtyard to both Hindus and Muslims; and the area covered by the Ram Chabutara, Sita ki Rasoi and Bhandar to the Nirmohi Akhara. The court deemed that the share of the Muslim group could not be less than one-third of the total area of the premises. The Bench observed: 'Once such belief gets concentrated to a particular point…it partakes the nature of an essential part of religion… Such an essential

[54]ibid

part of religion is constitutionally protected under Article 25.'[55] The verdict got challenged.

Earlier, among a string of orders, was one by a Civil Judge of Faizabad, in March 1951, under which jurisdiction Ayodhya falls. The judge said: 'It (further) appears from the copies of a number of affidavits of certain Muslim residents of Ayodhya that at least from 1936 onwards, the Muslims have neither used the site as a mosque nor offered prayers there and that the Hindus have been performing their poojas etc, on the disputed site.'[56] The opening of the locks happened in 1986 through a court order which was complied with by the Rajiv Gandhi regime. The District Judge had observed, 'It is clear that it is not necessary to keep the locks at the gates for the purpose of maintaining law and order or the safety of the idols. This appears to be an unnecessary irritant to the applicant and other members of the...community.'[57] A plea by a Muslim citizen seeking to stop the digging and levelling of land by authorities around the Babri mosque had been rejected by the Allahabad High Court in July 1992. The work had begun after the state regime had acquired that portion of the land. But after the mosque's demolition, the court struck down the state's notification for acquisition of the land and directed an end to all the ongoing work. Legalities and evidence apart, the Ayodhya issue became a test case for both Hindus and Muslims. The latter saw, in the destruction of the mosque, a blow to secularism, while the former interpreted the development as the coming of age of Hindutva—though not exactly in the way it panned out.

Would Tilak have approved of the demolition? Would even

---

[55]ibid
[56]ibid
[57]ibid

Savarkar have? On the other hand, should a mosque built by a foreign ruler—regardless of whether a temple was destroyed or not—be given primacy over the faith of millions of Hindus? Whatever version one may subscribe to, it seems to be a near impossibility for a mosque to now come upon the very same site it stood until December 5, 1992.

Acknowledgements

I have to begin by thanking columnist and author Atul Thakur for opening a window of opportunity, which enabled this book to be written. He had, months ago, suggested that I write a book, and when I took his advice seriously and mailed him a synopsis for a feedback, he was quick to do his bit. I am grateful also to Priyadarshi Dutta, a voracious reader on various subjects and occasional contributor to the print media, for having made available to me material that helped me shape the book. Besides, he offered me valuable insights on the subject—after I confided in him details of the book I was working on. Unfortunately, constraints of space and the need to remain focused on the book's core theme prevented me from fully exploiting the wealth of knowledge he gave. Dr Syama Prasad Mookerjee Research Foundation and its director Anirban Ganguly extended courtesy and cooperation to the fullest when I was in need of research material. Twenty years ago, Julie, a friend and sister-figure from my Goa days, had suggested that I write 'some book'. More recently, senior journalist and author Hiranmay Karlekar gently nudged me to make an attempt. I am thankful to them for having trusted my ability. Shreya Kedia, colleague and friend during my days at *The Pioneer*, too would, of and on, suggest that I write a book. Those days, she had more faith in me than I had in myself. A big 'thank you' to Shreya! I must also extend my gratitude to team members at Rupa Publications for their help throughout, beginning from accepting a proposal from a first-time author. I would like to especially thank the firm's commissioning editor, Rudra Narayan Sharma, for his guidance in crafting the book proposal in a way that made sense, both content-wise and commercially.

Through the months that I was engrossed in the project, I had turned even more non-communicative at home than I usually am. My wife Pushpa stoically put up with this irritating conduct, and even commended me for finally 'doing something meaningful in life'. The book took some toll on my financial affairs, since I had to discontinue my contributions to a bunch of online platforms, and thus suffer a monetary hit. In these challenging moments, my daughter Shikha and son Nikhil—and their respective families—stood by me and kept me afloat. Writing a book is a solitary exercise, and there were times when I felt lonely and despairing. In those gloomy moments, the presence of my grandchildren, Kavya and Vikrant, came as a ray of sunshine amidst the dark clouds. They are too young now to understand how much I owe them.

Bibliography

A Storm of Songs: India and the Idea of the Bhakti Movement; John Stratton Hawley; Harvard University Press, 2017

Academic Hindophobia: A Critique of Wendy Doniger's Erotic School of Indology; Rajiv Malhotra; Voice of India, 2016

An Introduction to Hinduism; Gavin Flood, Cambridge University Press; Reprinted in 2014

Ayodhya Revisited; Kishore Kunal; Ocean Books (P) Limited, 2016

Babri Masjid: A Tale Untold; Mohammad Jamil Akhtar; Genuine Publications & Media Pvt Ltd, Reprinted in 2017

Bhakti Religion in North India: Community Identity and Political Action; Edited by David N. Lorenzen; SUNY Press, 1995

Bodies of Song: Kabir Oral Traditions and Performative Worlds in North India; Linda Hess; Permanent Black; First Indian printing in 2015 by permission of Oxford University Press

Brothers against the Raj: A Biography of Indian Nationalists Sarat and Subhas Chandra Bose; Leonard A. Gordon; Columbia University Press, 1990

Bunch of Thoughts; M.S. Golwalkar; Vikrama Prakashan; Fourth Impression, December 1968

Communalism in Modern India; Bipan Chandra; Har Anand Publications, 2008

Complete Works of Sri Aurobindo (28 Volumes); Sri Aurobindo Ashram

Culture of Encounters: Sanskrit at the Mughal Court; Audrey Truschke; Penguin Allen Lane, 2016

Decolonising the Hindu Mind: Ideological Development of Hindu Revivalism; Koenraad Elst; Rupa Publications Pvt Ltd, 2007

Deendayal Upadhyay: Sampurna Vadmay (15 volumes); Prabhat Prakashan, 2016

Early India: From the Origins to AD 1300; Romila Thapar; University of California Press, 2002

Encyclopedia of Hinduism; Edited by Constance A. Jones & James D. Ryan; Facts on File Inc, 2007

Encyclopedia of Religion and Ethics (George Abraham Grierson); Edited by James Hastings; 1908-27

Gita Press and the Making of Hindu India; Akshaya Mukul; HarperCollins Publishers India, 2015

Half-Lion: How P.V. Narasimha Rao Transformed India; Vinay Sitapati; Penguin Viking, 2016

Hindi Sahitya ka Itihaas; Acharya Ramachandra Shukla; Prakashan Sansthan, 2016

Hindi Sahitya: Udbhav aur Vikas; Hazariprasad Dwivedi; Rajkamal Prakashan, Twenty-first Edition, 2017

Hindu Hriday Samrat: How the Shiv Sena Changed Mumbai Forever; Sujata Anandan; HarperCollins Publishers India, 2014

Hindu Mahasabha in Colonial North India, 1915-1930: Constructing Nation and History; Prabhu Bapu; Routledge, 2012-13

Hindu Nationalism and Indian Politics; Bruce D Graham; Cambridge University Press, 1990

Hindu Nationalism: A Reader; Edited by Christophe Jaffrelot; Permanent Black; Sixth Impression 2017

Hindu Rashtra Darshan; Veer (Vinayak Damodar) Savarkar; Abhishek Publications, 2012

Hinduism; Monier Monier-Williams; Pott, Young, & Co., 1878

Incarnations: India in 50 Lives; Sunil Khilnani; Penguin Allen Lane, 2016

India: A Sacred Geography; Diana L Eck; Harmony Books, 2012

Indian Religions: A Historical Reader of Spiritual Expression and Experience; Edited by Peter Heehs; NYU Press, 2002

Indianisation? What, Why and How; Balraj Madhok; S. Chand, 1970

Khaki Shorts and Saffron Flags: A Critique of the Hindu Right; Tapan Basu, Pradip Datta, Sumit Sarkar, Tanika Sarkar, Sambuddha Sen; Orient Blackswan, 1993

Lokmanya Tilak: Father of the Indian Freedom Struggle; Dhananjay Keer; Popular Prakashan, Third Edition, 2016

Mahakavi Surdas; Edited by Baldev Vanshi; Prakashan Sansthan, 2013

Makers of Modern India; Edited and Introduced by Ramachandra Guha; Penguin Viking; 2010

Marshalling the Past: Ancient India and its Modern Histories; Nayanjot Lahiri; Permanent Black, 2012

Merriam-Webster's Encyclopedia of World Religions; Edited by Wendy Doniger; Merriam-Webster, 1999

Mira Bai; Usha Nilsson; Sahitya Akademi, 1997

On Hinduism; Wendy Doniger; Aleph Book Company, 2013

Paanch Bhakt Kavi: Vivad aur Vimarsh ke Sandarbh Mein; Murli Manohar Prasad Singh; Bharatiya Jnanpith, 2017

Rama and Ayodhya; Meenakshi Jain; Aryan Books International, 2013

Rashtriya Swayamsevak Sangh; D.R. Goyal; South Asia Books, 1979

Reflections; Swami Vivekananda; Om Books International, 2018

Religion, Power & Violence: Expression of Politics in Contemporary Times; Edited by Ram Puniyani; SAGE India, 2005

RSS's Tryst with Politics: From Hedgewar to Sudarshan; Pralay Kanungo; Manohar Publishers and Distributors, Reprinted in 2017

Scholar Extraordinary: The Life of Professor the Rt. Hon. Friedrich Max Muller, P.C.; Nirad C Chaudhuri; Chatto & Windus, 1974

Situating Sri Aurobindo: A Reader; Edited by Peter Heehs; Oxford University Press, 2013

Surdas: Poet, Singer, Saint; John Stratton Hawley; Primus Books, 2018

Swami Vivekanand: The Living Vedanta; Chaturvedi Badrinath; Penguin Books India, 2006

Syama Prasad Mookerjee and Indian Politics; Prashanto Kumar Chatterji; Foundation Books, Revised Edition, 2015

The Ancient Indus: Urbanism, Economy, and Society; Rita P Wright; Cambridge University Press, 2010

The Battle for Sanskrit; Rajiv Malhotra; HarperCollins Publishers India, 2016

The Brotherhood in Saffron: The Rashtriya Swayamsevak Sangh and Hindu

Revivalism; Walter K Anderson & Shridhar D Damle; Vistaar Publications, 1987

The Construction of Communalism in Colonial North India; Gyanendra Pandey; Oxford University Press, 1990

The Discovery of India; Jawaharlal Nehru; Penguin Books India, 2004

The Embodiment of Bhakti; Karen Pechilis Prentiss; Oxford University Press, 2000

The Foundations of Indian Culture; Sri Aurobindo; Sri Aurobindo Ashram Publications Department, 1998

The Future of Indian Politics: A Contribution to the Understanding of Present-Day Problems; Annie Besant; Theosophical Publishing House, 1922

The God Who Failed: An Assessment of Jawaharlal Nehru's Leadership; Madhav Godbole; Rupa Publications India, 2014

The Hagiographies of Anantadas: The Bhakti Poets of North India; Winand Callewaert; Curzon, 2000

The Hindu Mind: Fundamentals of Hindu Religion and Philosophy for All Ages; Bansi Pandit; New Age Books; Reprinted in 2014

The Hindu Nationalist Movement and Indian Politics: The Origins and Development of the Bharatiya Jana Sangh; Bruce D Graham; Cambridge University Press, 1990

The Hindu Nationalist Movement in India; Christophe Jaffrelot; Columbia University Press, 1998

The Hindu Phenomenon; Girilal Jain; UBS Publishers' Distributors, 1994

The Hindus: An Alternative History; Wendy Doniger; Penguin Viking, 2009

The Hymns of the Rigveda; Ralph T.H. Griffith; Motilal Banarasidass Publishers, Reprinted in 2004

The Jana Sangh: A Biography of an Indian Political Party; Craig Baxter; Oxford University Press, 1967

The Khilafat Movement: Religious Symbolism and Political Mobilisation in India; Gail Minault; New York Columbia University Press, 1982

The Language of the Gods in the World of Men; Sheldon Pollock; University of California Press, 2006

The Life and Times of Dr Syama Prasad Mookerjee: A Complete Biography;

Tathagata Roy; Prabhat Prakashan, 2012

The Life of Hinduism; Edited by John Stratton Hawley & Vasudha Narayanan; Aleph Book Company, 2017

The Lost River: On the Trail of the Saraswati; Michel Danino; Penguin Books India, 2010

The Nationalist Movement: Indian Political Thought from Ranade to Bhave; Donald Mackenzie Brown; University of California Press, 1970

The Saraswati Flows On: The Continuity of Indian Culture; B.B. Lal; Aryan Books International; 2002

The Selfless Mind: Personality, Consciousness and Nirvana in Early Buddhism; Peter Harvey; Routledge, 2013

The Sole Spokesman: Jinnah, the Muslim League and the Demand for Pakistan; Ayesha Jalal; Cambridge University Press, 1994

The Transfer of Power in India; VP Menon; Orient Longman; Reissued in 1999

The Turbulent Years: 1980-1996; Pranab Mukherjee; Rupa Publications India Pvt Ltd, 2016

The Untold Vajpayee: Politician and Paradox; Ullekh NP; Penguin Viking; 2017

Tilak and Gokhale: Revolution and Reform in the Making of Modern India; Stanley Wolpert; Oxford University Press, Second Impression, 1991

Unfinished Innings: Recollection and Reflections of a Civil Servant; Madhav Godbole; Orient Blackswan, 1996

Vedic River Saraswati and Hindu Civilization; Edited by S Kalyanaraman; Aryan Books International, 2008

Vindicated by Time: The Niyogi Committee Report on Christian Missionary Activities; Introduction by Sita Ram Goel; Voice of India, 1998

Vivekananda: World Teacher; Edited by Swami Adiswarananda; Rupa Publications India Pvt Ltd, 2007

Who Invented Hinduism?: Essays on Religion in History; David N. Lorenzen; Yoda Press, 2006

Why I Am a Hindu; Shashi Tharoor; Aleph Book Company, 2018

Index